WIZARDLING

Michael J. Mayer

WIZARDLING

By
Dr. Michael T. Mayo

Queens Army LLC   Tucson, Arizona

ISBN # 978-1-940985-73-2

Library of Congress control # 2019903824

Published in April 2019

Published by: Queens Army LLC

2300 N. Craycroft Rd. # 5

Tucson, Arizona 85712

Our website is: queensarmy.net

Distributed by Ingram

Contents

"Wizardling" is the story of
Dr. Mayo's transformation
from sorcerer into a wizard.

Introduction

Dr. Mayo practices the ancient arts of Dream Walking and Shape Shifting. He combines these skill sets with Time Travel and the art of illusion for you in the "Wizardling". In this book you are given a glimpse of the power and magic that lies buried deep within the 'Realm of Infinite Possibilities' or what sorcerers otherwise call Wizard's Island. These stories were not fabricated. Dr. Mayo experienced all of these adventures that he is sharing with you now from beyond the 'Canyon' where 'Vishnu' the 'Dreamer' dreams his Dreams that create and sustain our physical reality.

The term 'wizardling' is used to describe a young wizard. It also describes a new wizard, for in the world of wizards, time is merely an inconvenience not a reality.

The main objective of sorcery is discovery, while the goal of wizardry is predictability. Anyone who seeks the Source can be called a sorcerer. Being called a sorcerer and actually being a sorcerer are vastly different things.

To acquire the status of 'Sorcerer' you must be able to reach the Abyss, leap into it and survive your leap into the unknown.

The difference between a sorcerer and a wizard is that the wizard passes over the abyss as a dis-embodied point of awareness, crosses over to the other side of the 'Canyon" and begins life as wizard, leaving behind life as a sorcerer. When a sorcerer becomes a wizard they acquire two protectors, an elf and a giant. They transition from active dreaming to converting dreams into reality. This is necessary to create predictability.

Dr. Mayo's Mantra

Nothing is what it appears to be, ever.

Don't take it personally, even if it's meant to be.

Every challenge brings an opportunity, the gift.

The secret is to focus on the opportunity...
*   Not on the challenge.*

Expect nothing, and you will never be disappointed.

The only thing between you, and your dreams,
*   is you.*

Give yourself permission to fail... So you can
*   give yourself permission to succeed.*

Treat yourself the way you want others to treat you.

Learn to say 'Thank You' and mean it.

Forgive others...
*   So you can forgive yourself.*

The Canyon

I first met Samuel Morse the morning of the 12th of November 2015. That was yesterday. He introduced himself to me as my 'Guide'. I ran into him again this morning for the second time, at 12:45 a.m. on the 13th of November, when I was returning from a quick trip to the bathroom. I asked Samuel if he might be interested in catching a flight of fantasy on the night plane, which was due to arrive, at 1:00 a.m. He said that he wasn't interested. Then, I asked if he might want to catch the 'Night Bus' that comes by at 2:00 a.m. or to maybe catch the 'Night Train,' which comes by at 4:00 o'clock sharp.

Samuel said that he wanted to take me to 'The Canyon'. So I agreed to go along with him. He showed me a door with the words 'THE CANYON' written on it in large block letters.

As he opened the door, we were sucked into the opening by some invisible wind. The door closed behind us on its own and then disappeared. We were two tiny dust specks floating across this giant canyon. It wasn't as large as the Grand Canyon but it was very deep, with both sides tapering down towards a ribbon of what appeared to be the shiny surface of water reflecting the image of the sky above.

Samuel appeared to me as a tiny dust speck, so I must have also been a tiny speck of dust myself. As we drifted towards the other side, Samuel asked me how far I thought it was to the other side of the canyon. I told him, it looked to me to be several miles, maybe three or four miles. That was my guess. He told me that what appeared to be the reflection of the sky above from the surface of water in a river at the bottom of the canyon, was in fact the sky. For this was not a canyon at all but the vertical sides of two separate worlds, where the great distance down the walls of the two worlds gave the appearance of tapering inwards towards its bottom but there was no bottom, only sky on the other side of 'The Canyon'. Samuel told me that the distance between these two canyon's walls was measured not in miles but in time…a life time… my life time.

The side that we left behind was 'before' we met on November 12th, for the first time. The other side of the canyon was when we finally arrived on the other side, wafted as two dust specks by the 'winds of change', on November 14th 2015, where we would become inseparable, my guide and I. The life and the world I left behind would no longer remain. The new life, the new world would be where I would exist for the remainder of this life, a place infinitely different than the life I had known before.

San Francisco

Last week the Source asked me to walk with him while we talked. He told me that he was surprised by the progress I have made thus far. As we walked through this darkened space filled with what looked like fog that swirled around us like smoke. He explained to me that he thought I was ready to encounter what sorcerers refer to as the abyss. We stopped at the edge of a cliff that was filled with pure blackness.

The Source explained that every sorcerer was expected at some point to reach the edge of the abyss and to leap into it. The sorcerer would then either survive or they would perish in that great leap. He took my hand and we walked out into the abyss, out beyond its edge. I looked over to where he had been moments before and he was gone. I looked down at myself and I too was not there, yet we continued our conversation as though nothing had changed. The Source wanted me to understand what the abyss actually was and by comparison he brought up the void and the place of emptiness. Both of these are actually places where you can go to but the abyss on the other hand is not a destination that you go to, like San Francisco but a place you depart from, like San Francisco. So, it turns out that the abyss is the place or point where you depart from physicality. Nothing physical exists in the abyss. Nothing physical exists in the place of emptiness, which is to your left and nothing physical exists in the void, which is to your right. Straight ahead lies the abyss. The world of the sorcerer ends in the abyss. The space where the art of sorcery is plied is called the dreamscape. Dreams in the dreamscape are created and populated by the sorcerer. Beyond the edge of the cliff is the canyon, which separates the world of sorcery from the world of wizardry. The world of the wizard begins on the other side of this canyon. Wizardry lies in the world of dreams, the dreams of Vishnu the dreamer. The objective of wizardry is to dream the dreamer and dream the dreamer's dreams, something a sorcerer can never do. When we reached the other side of the canyon the Source said, "You are no longer a sorcerer, you are now a wizardling."

Hannah

I opened my eyes and found myself gazing at a delicate white porcelain teacup that I was holding in my hand. It was beautifully decorated with miniature flowers and accented with a gold rim. It was filled with fragrant tea that I was preparing to sip. Close to my cup was another identical cup, also filled with that same fragrant tea, held up by a perfectly manicured female's hand with its pinky finger elevated, ever so slightly. The hand was that of an immaculately appointed woman appearing to be in her early thirties.

As we casually sipped our tea together she waved her hand slowly in a sweeping panoramic motion encompassing the richly decorated mansion where we were sitting, looking out from an elevated balcony at the perfectly landscaped property extending out to the shoreline in the distance. Then motioning to include herself she said, "All of this is yours for the asking."

She was truly a lovely lady. The mansion was magnificent and its manicured landscape was spectacular.

I asked her who she was. She revealed to me that her name was Hannah. Then, I asked her what she was. With my newly acquired wizardling powers of perception, I knew she was a devil in disguise.

My response was, "I have no interest in acquiring these things. I am searching for the understanding of things and the why of things and the what of things." Hannah and everything else instantly vanished. I asked the Source what the devil could possibly want from me. He said that the devil wanted my rings. They reappeared on my fingers when the Source mentioned them. Four rings on the four fingers of my right hand and the one ring on the index finger of my left hand that controlled them all. The Source said, "Sorcerers and devils can not use the powerful magic contained in these ancient rings. Only wizards have this ability. But, they still covet them and will do anything to possess them."

Sapphire

Last night, I sat down on the park bench overlooking the event horizon between the Facilitator on my left side and Sabatini on my right side. I asked the Facilitator if he would consider going with me to the other side of the canyon to see Wizardling Hall. He most emphatically said he would not ever go there. I asked him again if he were an angel or if he had ever been human or what he was exactly and how he became to be associated with me. He said that he was not even physical and he had never been human but he would not disclose any information about his past or how he became involved with me. When I asked Sabatini, the traveler's Buddha, if he would like to go with me to the other side of the canyon, he was very enthusiastic about going there to a place he had never been to before. I told him that we should probably go by portal because I didn't know if I would be able to cross over the canyon with him and not have a problem. I suggested that he get on my shoulders because I didn't want him to get lost in the crossing.

We went to my back yard and I opened a portal to the structure known as Wizardling Hall. We entered the portal with no problems but instead of us materializing inside of the great hall there was an explosion of some kind and then rapid-fire chaos. In the process I lost Sabatini and I was forced to return to our entry portal. I checked to see if Sabatini had made it back to where we had been overlooking the event horizon but he was not there. I knew then that I would have to go looking for him. I opened a portal to where he was and found him in the middle of a dense jungle. Neither he nor I had any idea how he ended up in the jungle instead of in Wizardling Hall. I told Sabatini that we needed to sit down on the jungle floor and figure out what had happened. While we were discussing several different possibilities, a tall hooded figure in a long robe appeared in an opening in the dense jungle.

When I revealed to the stranger what had happened

and that I was a wizardling he removed his hood and said that he was a wizard and showed us his gnarled staff with a very large sapphire jewel on the top. He said that he was known as the Sapphire Wizard because he was given this staff with the sapphire on it when he became a full-fledged wizard. I asked him what his name was before he acquired the status of the Sapphire Wizard. He told me his name was William. When I asked him about the jungle we were in he told me a strange story.

He said that a beautiful temptress had cast a spell on him and he ended up here in this dense jungle where there were no animals, birds or people and there was no way to get out. He had a very long gray beard and said that he had been here seemingly forever. It was always either dawn or dusk, for the sun never came up and the sun never set. It was as though time had stopped and the only indication of how long he had been here was the length of his very long, gray beard. He explained to me that soon after he had been promoted to full wizard a beautiful enchantress named Isabella invited him into her magnificent castle and promised him more than the Garden of Eden. They shared a glass of magical wine together and he woke up here in this jungle with no way out.

I told William the Sapphire Wizard that Sabatini and I might be able to get him out of this jungle but that we would all have to hold on to each other securely so that no one became lost in the process. I assumed that what happened when Sabatini and I attempted to transport into Wizardling Hall, was that we were prevented from entering because Sabatini is not a wizardling. Inside of the great hall it is stable but outside the hall there are all kinds of dreams transpiring simultaneously. Sabatini must have become stuck in a dream, this jungle dream, like the game Jumanji, the same dream that William the Sapphire Wizard was put into by Isabella the enchantress.

I opened a portal to the past into the castle of the enchantress at the moment they were making their toast and then opened the domed lid of the small magical box that stops time and switched their glasses. When the enchantress took a sip from her glass, she immediately passed out and fell to the floor unconscious.

I asked William to help me carry the beautiful temptress to her bedroom and we placed her on her bed. William proclaimed loudly, "Now I shall have my way with her!" I grabbed his sapphire staff from him and whacked him on the head with it as I yelled out, "You idiot!" Thenceforth he became known as the "Idiot" of Isabella the temptress and I assumed his identity as the Sapphire Wizard.

Balsamo

Questions that are unanswered leave situations unresolved. Looking for answers can take you to strange places and to even stranger encounters. I eventually ended up in the bedroom of the beautiful temptress

Isabella. I appeared out of thin air. Though we speak different languages, we communicated effortlessly via mental telepathy. In an effort to keep her off balance and off my trail, I opened the small box that stopped time frequently and moved freely to several other locations within her bedroom. Each time I closed the box and time commenced once again, I was in a different place.

I asked her if she knew of any spell that could break the hold that opium has on its victims or if she had any suggestions that might be beneficial in such a case. Isabella said, "You must interrupt their supply of opium. There is no other way to alter the outcome which is always death." I closed the box for the last time after I was far away from her castle deep within the forest where she could never track me or find my trail.

From there I sought out the maker of the 'sapphire staff' which I had recently taken from the Wizard William, who was now an 'idiot', Isabella's idiot. When I found him he was busy constructing that very sapphire staff far back in ancient time. His name was Jacamo. I asked Jacamo what he was making even though I knew exactly what he was making because I had stolen it away and taken it into the future. Jacamo said that he was creating a magnificent sapphire wizard's staff. I asked Jacamo what kind of wood he was using to make the staff and what could the staff actually do. Jacamo told me that this staff was made from the main branch of a young Balsamo tree from Peru. He said he was attaching a beautiful blue sapphire to its top and what it could do depended on the wizard who possessed it.

I asked Jacamo if I might hold this unfinished staff. His response was, "If you touch it, it will someday find its way back into your life."

The staff felt warm and smooth to my touch. It was surprisingly lite and beautiful to hold. I returned the yet unfinished sapphire wizard's staff to Jacamo, thanked him for the information and vanished back into the future from whence I had come.

Jasmine

Tuesday night we retired for the evening at around 9:15. I turned the lights off at 9:30. At 9:45 my wife said to me that something was in the room and had just touched her head. She wanted to know what it was and why it was there. These things always come to her side of the bed.

The first thing I do, in these situations, is to establish communication with the visitor and then ask whatever it is to come over to my side of the bed. It was short, less than four feet tall. It looked female because it had small features and long wavy blondish-brown hair and a slight build. Its ears were pointed and rather pronounced in size. She held a triangular shaped gold-colored thing between her two extended hands that resembled a truncated pennant flag with its narrow end pointing downward. I asked the thing if it were female and it said that it was. Next I asked it if it were a fairy and it again said yes. She told me that her name was Jasmine, a pretty name for a pretty little fairy. When I asked her why she was there and what she had in her hand she told me that my wife had injured her right knee and she had brought a magical bandage to put on her knee so that it would get better. Jasmine said that if she didn't put the magical bandage on my wife's knee it wouldn't get better but instead it would only get worse.

My wife twisted her leg while dragging a large birdcage from outside, back into the house right before dinner. I asked Jasmine how she knew that my wife had injured her knee. Jasmine said, "We keep track of her." The last question I asked her was if she could really fly. She said yes, then, she wanted to place the bandage on my wife's leg. It was about eleven inches wide and fourteen inches long tapering to the truncated end that was about four inches wide. I told my wife who was there and what she wanted to do and my wife said for her to go ahead and do it. As Jasmine departed, she said that she would come back and remove the magical bandage in two or three days. Then Jasmine disappeared into the night.

Later I went looking for Jasmine the fairy. I followed her trail to where it disappeared into the forest but no fairies ever appeared. Apparently they had no interest in talking with me.

Wizard's Robe

I woke up at 1:59 in the morning. I ran out to the front of the house as the Night Bus came to a stop. I climbed on board and showed Brad, the bus driver, my new wizard's staff with the big blue sapphire stone attached to its top and asked if he knew where I might get a wizard's outfit. He said that he did and we took a ninety-degree turn at the intersection then bounced down a long staircase in the tired old school bus. When we reached the bottom of the stairs we turned right and traveled a short ways before the bus stopped at the edge of a fast moving river about twenty or thirty feet wide. The water was moving really fast and it was quite turbulent. Brad said that there were elves on the other side of the river who would help me out. I got off of the bus and it disappeared as my foot touched the grass.

I knew there was no way I could swim across the turbulent river so I grasped the wizard's staff tightly and said to it, "Let's do this thing" and we floated up and over the river. On the other side was forest. As I walked through the forest I came up to a large tree with a trunk about two and a half to three feet in diameter. On the other side of the tree was a small village with a cobblestone street, lined on both sides with diminutive little cottages. Elves lived here. Three times I walked back to the other side of the tree and each time I did so the village would disappear, then it would re-appear when I returned.

In the village I encountered a small elf and asked if anyone there could make me a wizard's outfit. The first thing he did with out saying a single word was to measure my feet with a stick. He left the spot and returned shortly with a pair of elf looking shoes with the pointed toes turned up. They looked really weird to me but they fit perfectly and were extremely comfortable. They felt like I was wearing clouds on my feet. The next thing he brought out was a strange looking hat. It had a wide brim and a long pointed top that was all flopped over like a dead cat. Each item the elf brought matched the blue color of the sapphire on the top of the wizard's staff. Next he brought out some funny looking pants with bloomer type legs and an elastic cuff that fit tightly around my ankles. The elf twisted each pant leg around and around until it fit snuggly around each leg but looked bizarre all twisted up like a candy cane. The last item of clothing the elf brought out was a long coat with no collar. It may have had a hood but it certainly had no collar and no buttons. Instead it had loops made from some kind of strange plant or animal fibers woven together. All of these articles of clothing were the same color and made from the same heavyweight hand woven material that didn't look or feel like wool or cotton. It felt more like cashmere. I thanked the elf for his generous gifts but the elf never said a single word. He summarily turned and disappeared back into his tiny shop. It was much too small for me to enter.

Nunchaku

The full moon in September was at 12:06 a.m. on the 16th. This full moon was known as a 'Harvest moon,' which is the full moon that falls closest to the autumnal equinox that occurs on September 21st or 22nd of each year.

Every full moon magical crows bring me a gift. Last night I went out at 12:52 a.m. and there were four magical crows perched on the telephone wires in the alley behind my house. I sat down on the brick pavers near the swimming pool and they all flew down and landed near me. Each one of the crows had a fluorescent orange-colored, round stick in its mouth that was about a foot long and an inch in diameter. As I sat cross-legged on the bricks, each one of the crows approached me and bowed down and left its orange stick in front of me. I thanked them for the four sticks and asked what they were for. They told me that the sticks were magical and they could be used in many ways.

The head crow said, "If you place them together to form a square, they become a window into other dimensions and realities through which you can extract things and bring them back into our dimension and our own reality. If you place the four sticks end to end they form a magical walking stick. If you place them together to form a triangle they become a portal through which power can be transmitted into or out of another dimension or reality. When you place two of them together, they become two magical nunchakus. These weapons can be used against magical creatures in any dimension or any reality."

The nunchaku is the traditional Okinawan martial arts weapon we Americans call nunchucks.

Corridor

I checked in with the Source this morning at 4:30. He told me as we walked, to get dressed in the sapphire wizard's outfit and bring the sapphire staff with me and meet him in 'The Place'.

I dressed in the entire outfit including the white cashmere socks and the floppy hat and went to 'The Place' to meet up with the Source. I sat down on the silken smooth floor, placed the staff across my lap and quieted my internal dialog. When there was complete silence and pure darkness some sort of energy, like a wind, filled my entire outfit including the white socks and the floppy hat until they were swollen up like an air filled display at the grand opening of a used car lot. After a few minutes the rushing gas-like energy ceased coming into my wizard's attire and everything began to deflate slowly. The whole outfit was left somehow softened and thickened as though the material it was made of had been divided in half and left with some kind of filler in between the two layers. It felt like two layers of very soft material with tiny pliable bubble wrap left in between.

At this point the Source appeared and said that now I was ready. I asked the Source about what had just transpired. He said that every fiber of the natural material that the cloth was made of was now enshrouded with the same energy that created and sustains the universe. This material itself was now like a giant battery and a constant source of energy available for my use for personal protection and to achieve any of my desired objectives. At that moment a passageway appeared. Above the entrance that was a little less than eight feet high and six feet wide were the letters 'CORRIDOR'. It was like a long straight hallway lined with alternating doorways first to the right and then to the left, then right then left, that continued as far as the eye could see. I asked the Source how long the hallway was to get some idea as to how many doors there might be. The Source replied, "As long as you live."

I asked the Source in what direction the hallway was oriented. He said that it faced east at the moment but in reality it didn't have a direction. I turned around and faced in the opposite direction and the passageway faced due west. Whatever direction I faced the same passageway faced in that direction. When I asked what the point of the passageway was, the Source said, "It is for you to open every door."

The Source disappeared and I was left alone standing in front of the open passageway facing east. When I put my foot into the threshold of the opening to the passageway, all of the doors disappeared except the very first one on the right. When I withdrew my foot all of the infinite number of doors reappeared.

As I prepared to pass through into the tunnel, a braided white silk cord appeared across the entrance attached to either side. A small, embroidered message hung from its middle. It read, "Those who enter here, never return." I walked through the entrance way and the message and its silken cord both vanished.

Door number one

I wanted to see what lay behind the many doors within the corridor. When I stepped into the corridor, all of the doors disappeared except the very first door on the right. That door itself had no hinges and no doorknob. There was no keyhole and no visible way to actually open it. Observing the door with the aid of the rose-colored glasses was no help. Neither the double-lensed pince-nez spectacles nor the sword of truth provided any additional information about the door or how I could possibly open it. But by utilizing the wizard's powers of observation I was able to see into the door and understand how the locking mechanism could be activated by utilizing the magical key, given to me by the magical crows that could open any door, by inserting it into the center of the door and into an invisible keyhole. When I did so the door swung open easily and quietly. As soon as I stepped through the doorway I found myself standing in the middle of a really nice winding pathway. It was surrounded on all sides by a deciduous forest. There was nothing but lush vegetation as far as I could see.

I started off walking at a brisk pace because I wanted to see as much as possible before the sun set. I hadn't traveled very far before I sensed the presence of a second trail some 100 feet away running parallel to the path I was on. I decided to follow both paths at the same time. Shortly after that I sensed the appearance of a third trail some 100 feet on the opposite side of the trail I was traveling on. It was also running parallel to the path I was on. I decided to walk along on this trail as well. Walking down three different paths at the same time had taken many years of focused effort for me to actually accomplish it.

The three of me walked for quite a ways before the three pathways converged and opened up at the sales counter of a new car dealership in the parts department. The man behind the counter had three heads all wearing navy-blue baseball caps with the number 16 embroidered in large red numerals on the front of each cap. The three-headed man, standing behind the parts counter, was dressed in blue jeans and was wearing a white 'T' shirt with some kind of design silk-screened onto it. I didn't pay that much attention to what was on the shirt because my attention was drawn to the three heads of the man with their baseball caps positioned securely on their three separate heads, all dog's heads, all the same light-brown color, all the same breed of hunting hounds.

The three of me walked out into the empty parking lot at the car dealership and merged back into a single person, myself. I had no idea what the point of this exercise was waiting there for me behind that first door. I assumed that it was an exercise to demonstrate to myself or to others that I have mastered that particular skill set.

The thought occurred to me two days later when I saw Jose Fernandez' number 16 being worn by every member of his baseball team after he and two of his friends were killed in a boating accident in Florida at around 3:00 a.m. on the morning they were killed, that there may have been some connection with his death because of the number 16 and me having gone through that particular doorway at around 3:00 a.m. on that very same morning. Perhaps it was just a co-incidence.

But, I don't believe there is such a thing as a co-incidence. Everything is in some way is connected to everything else.

Door Number Two

Door number two was the first door on the left side of the corridor. As soon as my foot touched the floor when I stepped down into the corridor, all of the doors disappeared except the first door on the left hand side. When I pushed gently against this door, it opened easily and I found myself standing in the midst of a vast desert of sand dunes. The view with the aid of the rose-colored glasses was that of a vast desert of pink sand dunes. When I put on the double-lensed pince-nez spectacles it was transformed into a flat desert. The dunes were no longer there. With the reflection from the sword of truth, the scene turned into a wide valley.

But from the view with my newly acquired wizards perspective, there was a verdant landscape with a clear path beginning where I now stood, a wizard's path, the path I would follow into the future, my future.

Door Number Three

Later I returned to the corridor and once again stepped into the unknown. When my foot touched the floor on the other side of the entranceway, all of the doors disappeared but the second door on the right side. That door was the third door. I walked through it easily and this is what I encountered.

There was a darkened room with a string of memory balls hanging down on silk cords attached to the ceiling. I grasped one of the glowing memory balls with both hands. I was whisked into a nightclub and greeted with loud music and flashing lights from a disco ball. I recognized the woman sitting at the bar. She was downing one glass after another that was being served by an octopus. I moved closer and saw that the glasses being served were all filled with different colored pills. The octopus was the source for the pills she was taking. I opened the small box with the domed lid and time stopped. I grabbed the octopus that was supplying the pills and stuffed it into my leather pouch of suspended animation.

It may or may not help with the woman's drug problem but at least I took some action. Only time will tell if this action taken in my dream has in any way altered the otherwise imminent outcome of addiction to opioid drugs.

Fourth Door

The fourth door appeared to be identical to the previous three doors. Before I stepped into the corridor there were four doors. It was the second door on the left. After I stepped into the corridor, there was only one door it was on the left side. The power of the 'wizard's perception' allowed me to observe the inner workings of this door's locking mechanism. This lock had to be opened with a set of nine magnets. One round magnet was located in the center of the pattern. It was surrounded by eight rectangular-magnets. These magnets were arranged in a circular pattern around the central magnet with equidistant spaces between them. I would have never figured out how to open this door without being able to see through its thick metal covering using the wizard's powers of perception.

On the other side of the door there was total destruction from what appeared to be a nuclear blast. Nothing was left standing. Nothing was living there.

I first observed the devastation through the rose-colored glasses, then the double-lensed pince-nez spectacles and finally from the reflection in the sword of truth. The destruction was total and complete.

But, with the reflection from the sword of truth, a single flower came up from out of the blackened earth. It was a red rose. With the wizard's powers of perception, a large brown bear pulled the single red rose up out of the blackened earth and carried it away in its mouth.

I withdrew my mythical long bow from its sheath, knocked a magical arrow and shot it up into the night sky knowing with certainty that it would strike the heart of the bear. For Russia itself, was the instigator of this conflagration. Such is the nature of wizardry. Such is the nature of my magic.

Understanding Events

This morning a few minutes before one o'clock I asked the Source what I should be doing. He thought for a moment then said he thought I was ready to have a better understanding of events. He suggested I go to the year 1789 to Independence Square in the town of Philadelphia. I asked what day in 1789 and the Source told me that it should be today, October 4th in the year 2016. Then I asked about the time difference between here and the east coast. He said that it would be the same time there as it is here, one o'clock in the morning.

Right after I arrived at Independence Square in Philadelphia I heard the night plane approaching. It comes by at one o'clock sharp. I heard the clack, clack, clack, sound of a helicopter descending down from the sky. It landed right there in Independence Square and picked me up before taking off and heading out into the night sky finally leaving me at my house located in Tucson, Arizona.

The point of the whole experience was to help me grasp the concept that a scenario, any scenario, is comprised of a number of individual events that may or may not be sequential in absolute time or in place of origin. That is to say some or all of the elements that make up that scenario may be comprised of elements that are in fact imported into the scenario in order to alter the normal or expected outcome of that series of events.

In this particular scenario events from different places and different times were superimposed on one another to create an otherwise totally impossible scenario. Apparently this process of splicing events together is commonplace and is often used to create pre-determined outcomes.

Wizard's Island

A few nights ago I went out to catch the Night Bus at 2:00 o'clock in the morning. I asked Brad, the bus driver, if he could take me to the place where Wizardling's Hall was located but leave me at the 'back door' so to speak, if any such place actually existed. Brad told me he would leave me on the leeward side of Wizard's Mountain, which was sheltered from the onslaught of dreams streaming by from the windward side of the Island. He informed me that 'Wizard's Island' was a name often used by sorcerers when referring to 'the realm of infinite possibilities' that was for all practical purposes inaccessible to them. The place was not an island at all but was in fact infinitely large. The Night Bus dropped me off in a small sheltered area at the base of Wizard's Mountain. The dreamer's dreams were visible to me as they streamed past the mountain. I was isolated and safe as long as I remained hidden behind the mountain.

This morning at 3:50 a.m. something bounced onto our bed on my wife's side. I couldn't see what was there so, I asked it to come over to my side of the bed. This small creature that was about twenty-seven inches tall was standing next to the bed staring at me. I asked what it was, what it wanted and what its name was. The thing finally told me that it was an elf and that I could call it Jim. I asked it if its name were Jim and it said, no that was not its name but I could call it Jim. It said that every wizard has an elf. So I said that it was my elf. The elf responded saying that it was not my elf but on the contrary, I was its wizard. The Night Train was leaving and the elf said that it wanted to show me something. I instantly found myself in a vivid dream in full color. This dream lasted twenty-one minutes. In this dream, a lady that I know was in trouble. She gave me a hug and then she walked out the door of the office building and turned into a baby girl who proceeded to fall into my swimming pool in my back yard holding onto a small stuffed animal. I rescued her from the pool and kept her from drowning three separate times. The last time I turned away from the pool and carried her off to a safe place. The dream abruptly ended and I was back in my own bed and the elf was sitting on the bed next to me. I asked what that was all about and the elf said that it was my manager and it had allowed me to enter that dream to change the future for that lady. It was in fact the 'butterfly effect'.

I immediately found myself in another vivid dream in which I was in the neonatal intensive care unit of a hospital holding my youngest granddaughter. The head nurse wanted me to give the baby to an official baby holder but I refused and sat down in a rocking chair and insisted I would rock her until she was healthy before I would give her back to the nurses. The dream ended. The elf said that this too was the butterfly effect and I was altering the present by entering a vivid dream in the past.

I thanked the elf and asked how I should spell the name Jim. He said, "Call me Gem."

Full moon October 15th

This morning I awoke at 12:57 a.m. The raccoons came early last night and were running around all over the roof making all kinds of noise. I went out to our back yard to see if any magical crows had come around yet but there were none. I went out again to check for magical crows about an hour later. There were still no crows to be found. There was something that didn't feel right but I wasn't sure what it was. I assumed that something I was doing that was new since the last full moon might be interfering with the arrival of the magical crows. The only things I could think of was the arrival of Gem the elf or me spending more time on Wizard's Island.

I had left Gem the elf and the Giant on Wizard's Island last night when we transported over there together, so I returned to Wizard's Island and brought both of them back together with me. After that, the sky filled with hundreds of magical crows. They all descended into the yard and transformed into the Sorcerer's that they were. It looked like there were at least five hundred of them all shouting and cavorting excitedly congratulating me for becoming a wizard.

A short fat sorcerer emerged from the throng and began to speak above the uproar. He said that I was no longer a sorcerer but I was instead a wizard and therefore could no longer be 'King' of The Magical Crows. When I offered to return the golden crown they had given me he said that each crown was unique and should stay with its original owner. Each new king received his own personal crown at his coronation.

All of the sorcerers transformed back into magical crows simultaneously and became a veritable tornado of whirling black feathers and vanished. I was left wondering if this brought to an end their monthly gifts when there was a pop and a single magical crow appeared out of thin air and turned into a sorcerer. He apologized for having forgotten to give me the gift that he had brought in his excitement and hasty retreat. He then presented me with a parchment scroll tied securely with a golden cord. I thanked him and asked what it was for. He said that it contained the names of all the magical crows, all arranged in order alphabetically. He reminded me that I wouldn't even need to unroll it because I could use my wizard's power of perception to read the names inscribed there in.

Speaking of Others

Early this morning, sometime after midnight, I ventured into 'The Place' to recharge my energy supply. While there, I engaged the Source in a discussion about the Other. I asked the Source if it would be possible for me to bring my Other to 'The Place' and charge him up like I myself was being charged up. The Other is a duplicate of a sorcerer that is created by that sorcerer and is comprised of pure energy. It can be used by the sorcerer to accomplish tasks that would otherwise be too difficult or too dangerous for the sorcerer to do by their self. The Source said on the one hand that it would not be a problem for the Other that I had created to come and be charged up in 'The Place' but on the other hand wizards do not have Others but instead have a giant and an elf to assist them.

I was quite surprised to hear this but even more surprised by the response given when I asked what I should do with my Other. The Source said that the Other cannot exist without its creator. I had two choices. One choice was to allow the Other to no longer exist and the second choice was to integrate the Other into myself so that we became one entity instead of two. When I asked the Source how that could be done, he said that I was perfectly capable of accomplishing that by using the same technique that I had utilized in the past to re-assemble personalities that had for various reasons become splintered and separated.

It is true that in the past on several occasions I was confronted with fragmented personalities and I was able to unify these fragmented personalities by taking them all together through the "Door of No Return". They came out the other side as a single re-constituted personality. It is truly an amazing transformation.

I decided to give it a go and brought the Other over to 'The Place,' and charged him up. While he was being charged, we put the tops of our heads together so that his memory and my memory were identical before we went through the "Door of No Return". After going through the "Door of No Return" the Other became integrated with me and I presumably have acquired many of the powers of the Other.

Aurelius Buschard

I was awake this morning at 1:54 a.m. so I decided to try out the gift that the Magical crows gave me on the night of the last full moon. That gift was a rolled up scroll tied with a golden cord. Inside were the names of all the magical crows recorded in alphabetical order. I was told that my newly acquired wizardly powers of observation would allow me to read their names without even opening the scroll. When I tried it one of the names glowed, standing out from all the rest. It was Aurelius Buschard.

When the Night Bus stopped in front of our house at 2:00 o'clock I climbed on board intent on finding Aurelius. Brad, the raccoon bus driver, was sitting low in his seat with his cap pulled down low over his eyes like a 'low-rider'. I asked Brad what he was hauling tonight. He replied, "Two white rhinos. I'm taking them to Dream Time". The rhinos had made a complete mess of the interior of the old bus. The bus wobbled to and fro as the rhinos jousted about with each other in the back of the bus while Brad made his way to Dream Time. When we arrived in Dream Time the back of the bus opened and tipped down forming a ramp for the two rhinos to get down off of the bus. That is when I informed Brad that I wanted to go to see Aurelius Buschard. The bus floated slowly upward and seemed to evaporate leaving me in a clearing in a deciduous forest where a short man about five feet four inches tall with long hair and a dark beard was feeding the fire beneath a huge black caldron. I assumed that it was made of iron but it could have been made from clay.

As I approached the bubbling pot the man began to stir it with a giant wooden spoon. It looked like something you might use to paddle a canoe. I asked the short man if he were Aurelius Buschard. He nodded and asked if I wanted to stir the pot. As I stirred the pot, which was very difficult because it was so full, I asked him what was in it. He said, "Apples." I continued stirring for a very long time. When day began to break and the fire was spent and smoldering I asked Aurelius what he planned to do with all of these boiled apples. He told me he was going to let them cool for a day or two and then he would cover them with a cow hide and wait until they stopped bubbling, then he would jug them. It sounded like applejack to me. He was brewing up a huge batch of hard cider.

As the sun peeked above the horizon Aurelius took me to his house. It was a single room with a large fireplace at one end. There was a single entrance into the house. It had a solid wooden door with leather hinges. It also had two windows. Both were devoid of glass. Each window had a single shutter on the outside that covered the entire window opening and a second shutter on the inside on the opposite side of the window which also covered the opening completely. There was no kitchen, no sink, no running water, and no lights, not even a bed. In the middle of the room was a heavy wooden table with a couple of crude knives on it. A single heavy pot was hanging from an iron hook over the fire. It appeared to be iron but it also could have been a blackened clay pot.

Opposite the entrance into the single room was an opening with no door on it that allowed you to enter a storage area with wood walls on three sides and a low roof. To one side there was a mat on the floor. My guess was that was where he slept. On one side of the main room was a stair that led down into the cellar where there were row upon row of salmon colored jugs with corks sticking out of their tops. They were obviously for storage of his applejack. On the far side of the cellar, large chunks of dried and smoked meats hung down from the rafters that supported the floor above. After the tour of his house I asked him where the bathroom area was. He took me out to a large plot of green grass and said that was it. After that, I left Aurelius there but I returned several hours later looking for him.

I emerged into a room in a modern hospital. My guess was that it was in France, but it could have been somewhere else in northern Europe. The nurses were all speaking a foreign language but I understood everything they said in English.

Aurelius was in a hospital bed covered by a clean white sheet. He looked very old with his long gray hair streaked with black and his beard that was gray speckled by black. I went up close to his bedside and asked him, "How would you like some apple jack?" His eyes twinkled. I asked him what year it was where I had just left him in the forest. He said it was the year of our Lord 1247. He smiled at me then vanished. The nurses all began yelling and carrying on. They lost their indigent patient. They couldn't find him. Only I knew where he was.

He had traveled almost eight hundred years into the future to be treated in a modern hospital then, skipped out on paying his bill and returned to his home deep in the past where he was drinking applejack and kicking back in the year of our Lord 1247.

Absolute

Last night, before I went to sleep, I was talking with the Source. He said, "Walk with me." As we walked along side by side he instantly shrank to the size of a small mouse. I thought this was really weird. After a few more steps he became a huge giant many stories tall, before he finally returned to his normal size, which in itself is quite impressive. I was really quite surprised by the whole experience and so I asked him what that was all about. He of course asked me what was what all about. When I shared my experience, with him being tiny one minute then gigantic the next he replied, "I am the source of all things. I am the alpha and the omega. I am unchanging. I am the absolute. I have not changed in the slightest. It is you who first became gigantic thinking I had shrunk to the size of a mouse. Then you became extremely small and thought that I had become a giant. It is not I that changed size but you who have changed your size. You must contemplate upon that which has just transpired." With that he disappeared and left me standing alone in the darkness to sort out what had just occurred. I went to sleepwhile thinking about this recent encounter with the Source.

I woke up at 12:58 a.m. and decided to go out to the street in front of our house and wait for the night plane to fly over at 1:00 o'clock. I stood directly under the street lamp so that the pilot of the night plane would be sure to see me. I was surprised that I was unable to hear the night plane coming and disappointed that it hadn't arrived by 1:00 a.m. At 1:02 I started to go back inside the house when this model of a flying saucer silently slowed to a stop right in front of me. It looked to be about three or four feet in diameter and was floating at most three feet above the ground. It was not making any sound. I had no idea what could make it float like that. The color was a medium gray. When I touched it I could feel it sort of humming inside. The surface felt like it was made of some kind of ceramic metal composite. Its surface was warm to the touch but not actually hot. Using my wizard's powers of observation, I could see inside the craft. There were about eighty to maybe a hundred tiny little people walking around inside the spacecraft.

The next moment I was standing on the ground looking up at this giant flying saucer hovering above me that was several hundred feet in diameter. I transported myself up into the ship and was greeted by humans wearing plain body suits that all had a single decal on the right side, where a shirt pocket would normally be. It looked similar to the Nike symbol and was a dull red almost maroon. The rest of their attire was dark blue. Even their foot-ware was that same dark blue. There were no collars on their outfits and no signs of rank anywhere.

I engaged one of the humans in conversation. I asked him what year it was. He told me that it was the year 2784. The young man extended his hand in a gesture to shake my hand. I told him that I was a time traveler from the year 2016 and it would not be a good idea to make physical contact for either of us.

Later I re-engaged the source in conversation and asked him about what had just happened. He told me that even though I had mastered the ability to transport to anywhere and to any time, I still needed to work on the materialization in that place and time because I was obviously having difficulty getting my physical size correct. In jest I said, "Are you absolutely sure?"

Baldwin

Last night the Source told me that he thought it was

time for me to re-visit the dwarf Baldwin and introduce him to the Sapphire Wizard. He suggested that I make a point of arriving during daylight hours instead of the dead of night like I had a bad habit of doing. It is true that because I depart in the dead of night doesn't mean that I have to arrive at the same time because the actual time where I arrive could be very different from my own time. The second point I had been advised to work on was my physical size. So, I decided to arrive during daytime and I decided before departing how large I would actually be when I arrived. Since I am five-feet six inches tall, I decided that I would flip that and arrive being six-feet five inches tall instead. The Source wanted me to introduce Baldwin to the Sapphire Wizard, so I went dressed as the wizard in sapphire blue carrying the wizard's sapphire staff.

When Baldwin opened his door to greet me dressed as a strange wizard, he almost collapsed on the spot. I tried to reassure him but the combination of what I was wearing and me being almost a full foot taller with a long gray beard was overpowering anything that I could say to convince him otherwise. Eventually after I shrank myself down to my normal size and reminded him of all of the many adventures we had shared he finally acknowledged that I was indeed who I claimed to be. I told him that I was willing to become their wizard if he and his neighbors and family wanted me to assume the job of local wizard. Baldwin thought it might be helpful since their wizard had disappeared generations ago.

Before Baldwin summoned his neighbors to meet me I resumed my six-foot five inch stature. When everyone was present and they had agreed for me to become their wizard I told them I wanted to introduce some of my companions to them.

First I brought the elf and introduced him as the Sapphire Wizard's Elf, then, I brought the wizard's Giant, then the giant lion, then Sabatini and introduced him as the holy man that accompanied me on my journeys. Next came Khan the Great and his equally giant horse Phillip and his companion dog Peaches the Cardigan Welsh Corgi. Last but not least I introduced Lucky the six-year old boy whom I said was my wizard's apprentice.

This whole adventure began at 2:45 in the morning and was completed by 3:08 a.m. not too bad for a fledgling wizard.

Gondola

I went out in front of our house where the street lamp is located this morning at 3:00 a.m. to see if anything was going on. There was a large canal, where our street should have been. It was like one you would see in Venice. Parked next to the edge of the canal right in front of our driveway was this huge thing I will refer to as a gondola, though it was quite different from gondolas I have seen in pictures. It was much, much larger. The gondolier was standing on a platform on the back end of the gondola that was on the right side from where I was standing. There was a young woman dressed in white sitting at the opposite end of the gondola facing me. That would have been to my left. I climbed into the gondola, which had to be at least ten or twelve feet wide. That would have made the gondola at least sixty feet in length. As I walked along the flat floor, the gondola began to move slowly towards my right. We were moving eastward carried away by the invisible current of the canal.

The girl motioned for me to sit down next to her and engaged me in conversation. She was wearing a long white dress with long sleeves. It was an elaborately decorated dress for a party or formal affair. It reminded me of a bridesmaid's dress but could even be dressed up and used as a wedding gown with appropriate accessories. She introduced herself to me as Robin.

I asked her how old she was. Robin said that she was twenty but after a brief pause, she said that she would be twenty in twelve more days. Her birthday would be on November the eleventh. That was what convinced me that she was my Robin now reincarnated. I told her that I really didn't understand how that whole process of re-incarnation works. I thought you wouldn't remember anything from your past life after you began your next life. She smiled and giggled a little and said that she would try to explain it to me. I replied, "You are young and beautiful but I am old and getting ready to check out."

"No you're not. You are the same age as me. You

are twenty years old now. You will be twenty-one on your birthday in January." I looked down at my hands and sure enough they were like they had been in the past many years ago. Robin looked up at me and said, "I told you I would come to see you when I could. Don't forget, I'm your forever friend."

The giant gondola drifted backwards slowly down the canal as we reminisced, two forever friends together once again.

Gondola Girl

The giant gondola comes by in front of my house every morning at 3:00 a.m. Every time I venture out at 3 o'clock in the morning the gondola is there in front of the house waiting for me. Sometimes if I am a couple of minutes late, it is still there waiting. The girl in the gondola turned out to be Robin by another name. Last night or more correctly this morning she asked me to look deeper into the connections that have connected us through time. I had never really given that any thought. I had assumed that our relationship was just another cosmic oddity. The year is 1784. The place is Venice. Her name is Maria. She is twenty years old. My name is Valentino. We have a three story stone house or apartment overlooking the canal. Transportation is by gondola. The front door opens into the kitchen, which has a large open-hearth fireplace where all of the cooking is done over an open coal fire.

This area is very rough and quite dark with only one small open window of sorts, which allows for a draft of fresh air to enter to feed the fireplace. On the left wall of this single room there is a stone stairs leading up to the second floor, which is again a single room with an open fireplace directly above the fireplace below sharing a common chimney. This is the living room or sitting room as it were. On the right wall there is another stone stairs leading up to the third floor that also has an open fireplace fueled by coal. This is the bedroom. It has a single window like the sitting room. Both windows are covered by heavy drapes to keep out the cold of winter but are left open in warm weather. This is where we live. I have yet to find out what I do for a living. I think I am a merchant of some kind and travel frequently to other places to procure goods for sale or distribution and re-sale.

Our clothing is period appropriate but quite uncomfortable and bothersome to wear.

Charlotte

Last night on December 3rd, 2016 I hopped a ride on the 4:00 o'clock, Night Train. When the conductor asked where I wanted to go I told him I needed to meet up with Charlotte. We have never met before but I thought it might be possible to do so on the Night Train. I have been working on putting the book "Robin" together for her before her birthday next year in November as I promised to Robin. I transcribed the book twenty years ago but I have been dragging my feet but for a very good reason. The transcriptions were done in block form with no punctuation and no sentence separations. The biggest problem is that it is all in Elizabethan poetic form and I'm not a poet.

The conductor scratched his head, looked all around but I was the only one standing there under the street-light, then he yelled "All aboard". He told me to wait for the observation car to come by. It was the last car on the train. By the time the last car was getting closer the train was already moving pretty fast so I didn't wait for the last car but instead got onto the train a few cars before it. I only had a few cars to go through to get to the observation car, which was the twenty-first and last car on the train. I sat down at a small table for two and waited. It wasn't long before this nice looking young blond woman approached. She was wearing a winter coat with some kind of fur around its collar. I suggested that she would be more comfortable if she removed her coat but she sat down across the table and stared at me in a confused state. I asked her to place her hands on the table palms up and I placed my hands on top of hers. I then proceeded to show her a series of faces of boys and men. She looked at me very puzzled. I told her that they were all of my past and future incarnations. Then I showed her a series of girls and women's faces. I explained to her that they were all of her own past and future life experiences. Then, I paired them all up and showed her the images of each of the pairings. She was baffled by what she had just seen.

I explained to her that she was in the dreaming state and could remember this experience in great detail if she chose to do so but that would be entirely up to her.

Red Devil

Last night I asked the Source what he thought about me trying to do an exorcism on a person I thought might be possessed by some demon. The Source told me that would be a very bad idea and to just forget it. I took his advice but I felt that I should try to do something. What I decided to do was to go to the top of Wizard Mountain and intercept the streams of dreams that were connected to this person to see if that would alter the inevitable. After identifying the threads I began to cut them one by one.

When only one single thread remained intact, a rather impressive red devil with good sized ram's horns hurried up to me and offered to make a deal if I didn't sever the last dreaming thread. I told the devil that I didn't make deals with devils and severed that last thread. Only time will tell if that made any difference in averting the inevitable downfall of that person.

After that encounter, I also went to visit Merlin the magician who has been in Ireland for several years renovating the Glen and reviving its forests and fauna.

I of course appeared as my usual normal self otherwise there is no telling what Merlin might have done to me. When I told him about my recent accomplishments, he became very excited and enthusiastic about me becoming the new official wizard of the Glenn that he had just finished restoring. I told him I would be returning with all of the animals and other characters I could muster as soon as possible so that we could restore the magical world of Ireland to its former beautiful state.

Canary Road

Last night I was conversing with the Source when he told me he thought that it was time for me to return to the tenth attention and rescue those unfortunate souls hopelessly trapped there and unable to escape.

I reminded the Source that he had warned me to, "Beware...beware" and told me that it was not possible for me to help the people trapped there in the tenth attention. Later he reiterated that it was a hopeless situation.

Now all of a sudden he wanted me not only to go back to the tenth attention but also to rescue all those people hopelessly stranded there. The most bizarre thing about those trapped there was that they were all alive but their minds were entrapped in the tenth attention. They were for all practical purposes real live zombies.

After the Source asked me to go to the tenth attention and rescue all those hopelessly trapped spirits he departed leaving me to work through his request and create a successful strategy.

The first thing I did was to ask the Facilitator what he thought about me going to the tenth attention to rescue all of those zombie spirits trapped there. He thought that it was a very bad idea and told me not to go. Next I asked Sabatini the traveler's Buddha what he thought about me going there. He also thought it was a bad idea to go there and advised me not to go. Then I asked the wizard's elf what he thought about going to the tenth attention. He said there was no way he was going to go there and then vanished from sight. The last person I asked was the wizard's giant. He said he would go, no questions asked. I told him that the night bus would be coming soon but he would have to ride on the bus, not in the bus because he was so large. The giant said that it wouldn't be a problem for him to ride on the bus instead of in it.

But, subsequently I decided that there would be too much unknown risk if I took anyone with me. I needed to go alone. I also didn't want to risk loosing any of the many 'tools' I had collected through the years. So, I went with nothing but the leather thong that Aru the Aborigine keeper of Dream Time had given me as a gift years ago.

The Night Bus arrived a few minutes later. When I climbed on board Brad the bus driver gave me a weird look. I asked Brad what he was hauling on the Night Bus today. He told me canaries. The bus was full of yellow canaries. They were everywhere. I asked Brad where he was taking all these canaries. He said, to the coalmines. I asked him why he was taking all these pretty yellow canaries to the coalmines where it was dark and dirty. Brad said that when the canaries dropped dead, the coal miners knew it was time for them to get out of the mines because there was methane gas present. It was invisible, odorless and deadly and they had to get out of there in a hurry or they too would die.

When I told the bus driver that I needed to go to the tenth attention, he said, with a frown on his face, that he would drop the birds off first and then take me to the tenth attention. I told the canaries that if they went with the bus driver Brad to the coalmines they were all doomed to die a terrible death but if they went with me to the tenth attention there was a chance that they might survive. They all decided to take their chances with me much to the bus driver's consternation. As we made our way to the tenth attention, I asked Brad how many canaries were on the bus. My guess was about ten thousand. He said there were twelve thousand yellow male canaries. Those are the ones that sing constantly. They were all making so much racket that I told them if they wanted me to try to save them, they would have to follow my orders and do exactly as I said. My first order was for them to be quiet. When we arrived at the tenth attention I told the canaries to stay together and wait there for me while I surveyed the situation from above where all the humans were trapped, to see what was trying to catch them.

There were three giant creatures dredging with their long curved fingernails that were concave and would hook and scoop up the human spirits that were thrashing around hopelessly beneath the surface of what we might think of as a shallow sea. These creatures were hundreds of feet tall. I really needed to think up a scheme and think it up fast before we all would become lost souls in this dreadful place.

The Source has asked me to do many seemingly impossible things when he thought I was ready. He never told me how to accomplish these tasks but he always provided the things needed to get the job done but it was always up to me to figure out the puzzle before my time had run out. How could these puny yellow canaries save the day because I was no match for these three giant creatures with nothing but a leather thong.

Eureka! Then I made the connection. The source used the term hopeless several times in reference to these lost souls. They had all put themselves into the tenth attention by the decisions that they had made and it was hopeless for them to get out by themselves. That was it. That was the answer.

Miners in a coalmine were all hopelessly doomed to die from deadly methane gas. Their only hope came from these little yellow canaries. When the canaries stopped singing it was time to get out of the mines. These tiny yellow songsters would bring the gift of hope to these hopelessly lost souls. I told the canaries to each go to one of the people there and sing them their song and as they did so, each of the people vanished and returned to the world of the living to resume their lives. They were no longer zombies but normal functioning people. These puny little yellow canaries had given them hope.

Clickity Click

After rescuing all of the twelve thousand zombies from the tenth attention. I asked the Source what he thought of my solution to his challenge. He smiled a little, then said 'Good'. He then launched into his next challenge for me. He said that it was time for me to learn how to move sideways from one position to another location instantaneously. He said the method I had been using created too much distortion in the fabric of time. What I was doing was opening the small wood box with the domed lid and time stopped in a small area. That would allow me to move from one place to another place several feet away, then I would close the box and time would resume once again. The Source then went into some long discourse about getting outside of the stream of time then re-entering the time stream in another place, yadi, yadi, yadi and I was completely lost and fell asleep. But, the challenge remained.

When I woke up, I was in this strange place where there was a layer of what looked like a solid cloud of smoke right above my head. I reached up and put my hands into the layer of smoke. When I did that, a rope ladder fell out of the smoke. It had wooden rungs about fourteen inches apart and maybe eighteen to twenty inches wide. I climbed up into the smoke. It was very dense but only about nine inches thick. Above that I could see what looked like a sunset or sunrise on earth but the horizon was flat and the sun itself was strung out horizontally instead of being a round ball. It looked really different to me. I somehow made a click sound and I was instantly moved about nine feet to my left. I made another click and I was moved back to where I was originally located. I tried to repeat the process and made a clickety-click and I instantly went twice as far, about nineteen feet. I did this several times and saw that I was able to move in any horizontal direction at will and one click would get me nine feet and two clicks would get me about nineteen feet.

I remembered that during the Vietnam conflict, the soldiers used the term click or klick in reference to distance on a map. So many clicks to this place so many clicks to that place. That term was used in lieu of kilometer. In my mind there was some connection to sixteen but I'm not sure where that came from. There was something hazy in front of me it looked like a curtain made of some kind of fabric woven out of nylon rope. The rectangular spaces between the rope-fabric were the same dimensions as the openings in the rope ladder. That was about twenty inches wide and fourteen inches high. I climbed up the rope ladder and looked down on the top of the fabric. It was sinusoidal. The distance between two crests was about nineteen feet or sixteen of these openings and the distance between a crest and a trough was about nine feet or eight of these openings. This fabric turned out to be the Akashic curtain, the fabric of time. I could move in any direction instantaneously one click at a time or clickety-click nineteen feet at a time without causing a disturbance in time.

Cast About

Last night I was conversing with the Source as we walked along together. He has been walking with his hands clasped behind his back of late, so I did the same. I didn't need to share my story of how I had managed to go from one location, point A, to another place, point B, instantly, outside of time without relying on the little domed box to stop time for me. He already knew that. I could also tell that he was pleased and a little bit surprised that I had also managed to liberate the twelve thousand souls imprisoned in the tenth attention without any losses.

He began his tutorial by explaining the difference between possibility and probability. He said anything is possible and as such can occur everywhere and anywhere. It has no specific location where it can occur therefore it has no identifiable address associated with it. Probability on the other hand has some numerical coefficient associated with it, which is usually expressed as a percentage. Probability is used to predict an event or a time or a location it therefore has a specific locater associated with it. That in essence becomes an address as to where and when something might happen. To build on this lesson he told me that the three gigantic creatures in the tenth attention had the ability to predict where and when a person that departed from point A, would pop up instantaneously at another point B, therefore, it was imperative that I master the skill of popping up at two or more different points all simultaneously outside of time like 'whack-a-mole' and I was it.

I asked the Source what those three giant creatures actually were. I had never seen anything like them before. They were at least a hundred feet tall, maybe even a hundred and twenty feet tall. They had huge club like feet and giant hands with long curved scooping nails that they used to capture humans from beneath the surface of some kind of liquid that was almost eight feet deep. He told me they were ghouls.

The Source wanted me to return to the tenth attention and practice popping up simultaneously in more than two places at the same time. The ghouls were not capable of knowing where that third location would be. When I asked him exactly where the tenth attention could be found he told me that it was located between dreaming and being awake. It was the region you sensed as falling as you went through it.

With that information I ventured out to catch the Night Bus at two o'clock in the morning for a quick trip to the tenth attention. I asked Brad, the bus driver, what he was hauling today. He said he was delivering 'Cast Abouts' to the plain of re-assignment. I had been there a couple of times in the past and it was always interesting to observe. I asked exactly what were 'Cast Abouts'. Brad said they were male veterans who were homeless. I asked if they were all dead. Brad said that there were some dead and some undead. I was not exactly sure what he meant by the term undead.

When we arrived at the plain, which looked like the Bonneville salt-flats in Utah, all of the dead and undead filed off of the bus ahead of me. I told Brad that I would just tag along to see what was happening. Brad told me that I would have to leave all of my memories with him on the bus for safe keeping or the Assignment Angel would know right away that I wasn't dead.

I took Brad's advice and left all of my memories there with him on the bus and followed the line as it snaked its way towards the Assignment Angel. This Angel is very tall. It operates mechanically and tosses the veterans either to the right or to the left or hands them a scroll with their new assignment for their next incarnation. As they accepted their scrolls they took one step then just vanished. The undead were tossed into one pile that was to my right and the ones who had to return to earth because they had not completed their work were tossed into a pile on my left. When I finally reached the front of the line, the Assignment Angel recognized me from the last time I was there and with a startled look on her face she disintegrated into a thousand shards and I was left standing alone on the great flat desert plain. From there Brad took me to the tenth attention where I practiced simultaneously popping up in multiple places in a crazy game of 'whack-a-mole' and I was it.

Global perspective

Last night I was talking with the source. He told me that it was time for me to be able to observe the world from a hemispherical perspective, like in a planetarium or using a fish eye lens. He wanted me to acquire the ability to observe the world from every direction simultaneously. He said that to actually accomplish that feat I would have to engage all twelve eyes at the same time. Then he explained what he was referring to when he said all twelve eyes. That would be two normal eyes from each of the four cardinal directions plus the third eye from each direction totaling twelve. Sort of like a compound eye from an insect. I really had no idea how I might possibly be able to accomplish that trick.

Later when the night plane was coming by at 1:00 o'clock I ventured out to the street in front of our house to await its arrival. I waited for the sound of an airplane to approach but there was nothing, no sound, no plane, no nothing. I was ready to go back inside when an apparatus attached to a single cord was lowered onto my head. It was reminiscent of a helmet that

I once encountered in a very advanced aircraft some time ago. When it was secured in place I could see in any direction 360 degrees. This was what I needed to accomplish in a global way. I decided to go to Wizard Island and attempt to accomplish this feat there inside the cave where I would be isolated and protected from harm. I sat down in the middle of the cavernous space and began to meditate.

Out of the sky above me dropped this dome like bowl suspended by a single wire. I put it on my head and was then able to see in all four cardinal directions simultaneously. It helped me to make the transition from seeing in only one or two directions to being able to see in all four directions at the same time.

It took some effort but eventually I was successful and managed to see in a global way in every direction simultaneously with what appeared to me to be a seamless integration of all the different fields of vision.

When I discussed this personal advancement with the Source he told me that there were actually twenty-seven separate perspectives in the global view of reality. That's a lot of slices to splice together at the same time. I obviously need to do a lot more work on this process.

Gazing

The next night after accomplishing the task of seeing from a hemispherical perspective, the Source said it was time for me to re-visit the art of 'gazing'. Gazing is a process of using your eyes to gather information about something that is much more intrusive and inclusive than what you can gather by looking at the external appearance of something. It is an important tool used by sorcerers to accomplish many different things.

I was instructed to practice gazing on Wizard Island inside the conical hollow Wizard Mountain where it would be safe from all of the many things transpiring outside this cavernous space. I had been here a few years ago but I had no idea what it was or that it was located on Wizard Island. I didn't even know that such a place even existed. At that time I referred to this place in 'King on the Mountain'. I will repeat that experience for you here as either a reminder if you have read it in the past or as a reference to the spiral process by which I eventually gain a broader perspective of something when I eventually re-visit it.

My first efforts at gazing were with small inanimate objects. I worked my way around my environment there inside the cavern, before I worked my way outside of the safety of the hollow mountain. I sat and gazed out through the large opening where the dragons had entered the mountain on the lee side of the mountain. From that vantage point I could see the myriad threads streaming past that were sustaining physical reality. I also learned through gazing that the threads were not continuous but in fact coded information either attached to these threads or streaming down them incrementally at a very rapid rate. I was observing the future becoming the past.

While investigating the interior of this realm within the mountain, I came upon the sword and armor that I had donned when I was here years ago. I learned through gazing that these items belonged to the King of Titans. From that I surmised that this must have been where Titans once lived. That means that Titans must have been more than mythical creatures but powerful users of magic. There were none here now so something must have happened to them sometime in the past.

Over time I worked my way out of the mountain and up its steep sides, all the way up to its top. By becoming a pinpoint awareness and engaging the 360-degree global perspective I was able to see into the oncoming threads of reality. By moving outside of time instantaneously I observed not only the source of reality streaming straight up out of its origin but also how and where it was bent ninety degrees by time. Beyond this eruption of reality lay the engine of creation spewing something into this sea of threads and bending them ninety degrees and imbuing them with time.

After sharing my experience with the Source he told me that I had witnessed the dreams emerging from the Dreamer, the source of all physical reality and I had located the engine of creation. It was now time for me to try my hand at creation. Since I was now the only living wizard, the Sapphire Wizard. I needed to create a pattern, a mold and energize it with emotion. I told the Source that I had no idea how to create a mold or even what a mold was made of but the answers must be here somewhere on Wizard's Island.

Residence

Last night the Source told me that I would need to establish residence in or on Wizard Island to continue the process of becoming a full fledged wizard. He also said that I should take the elf and the giant with me. I didn't even know what their given names are but I hoped to at least get that much personal information about them.

After having a protracted discussion with the elf regarding his name it was finally settled that he would be called the 'Sapphire Wizard's Elf' by others but I was to call him 'Elf'. During our discussion of his title the question of how to get both he and the giant over to Wizard's Island as well as where they would be free to roam in safety while they were there.

Elf suggested I try a hemispheric transport mechanism to get them over to the island across the chasm between here and there as opposed to using other techniques. The technique I use for myself involves awareness only followed by reconstituting self on the other side. This won't work to transport others.

Portal to portal transport also has many limitations and drawbacks when attempting to transport something or someone across the void. I was not familiar with hemispheric transport but with help from the elf I was eventually able to move both the elf and the giant across the divide and into the hollow space inside of Wizard Mountain.

Fortunately or unfortunately for them, they have to remain inside of the protective space there inside the hollow mountain. They are not free to roam outside of this space.

In the end the giant wanted to be known as the 'Sapphire Wizard's Giant' and he wanted me to just call him giant. So last night all three of us changed our primary residence to 'Wizard Island' by using what Elf refers to as hemispheric transport. This is a process that is new to me but seems to have unique possibilities. Apparently elves have mastered this process and prefer to travel by the use of this method.

Alex

I was successful in bringing one Titan to Wizard Island. The name she gave me was Aurora. After she was settled in and sharing specific details about Titans I asked her if she was ready for me to attempt to bring another Titan to Wizard Island. She said that she wanted someone near her own age, which was twenty annums. That is the same as twenty years for us. Her specifications were for that someone to be beautiful and accomplished. What that means to her may not be what it means to me. From what she revealed to me, Titans are very large, on the order of ten to twelve feet tall. They live one to two thousand years and only live on Wizard Island. There are two genders and their reproductive cycle is not dissimilar from that of humans. Two limiting factors are that they only live on Wizard Island and Wizard Island only exists when there is a wizard in residence. No wizards means no Wizard Island. Ergo, there would be no place for Titans to live. The only viable option for me to acquire more Titans was to go back into the past when there were wizards living on Wizard Island.

I traveled back in time intent on finding another living Titan. The specific time period where I arrived was unknown to me. I encountered three wizards. They wanted to know who I was and what I was doing there in their world. My story did not sit well with them even though I was dressed in the attire of the sapphire wizard wielding a beautiful staff with a large sapphire crystal on top of it that was as blue as blue can be. Only after I manipulated time and appeared in different places simultaneously and gathered all of their wizard's staffs together and placed them next to mine, out of their grasps, were they open to my inquiries. After that and only after performing that unlikely feat, did Titans begin to re-appear. The only Titans that appeared were all young warriors. They lined up in a row facing me in an adversarial formation. There were twenty to thirty of them.

When I explained to them that I had come from the future to bring one beautiful male Titan back with me to be with a female Titan of twenty annums and that Wizard Island would cease to exist for them at some point in the future, five large impressive specimens stepped forward. The others remained in a single row staring out at me.

I asked each of the five strong young Titans to demonstrate for me their skills. Each of the five went through defensive and offensive maneuvers in turn one after the other. They were the five largest and most aggressive looking of the lot. What impressed me would not necessarily impress Aurora the female Titan residing with me on Wizard Island, far into the future.

I surveyed the entire lineup trying to imagine what Aurora would choose from this array of male Titans. I asked one of the males in the back row to demonstrate his skills for me. He stepped forward and began his slow methodical movements. They were more fluid, more deliberate and more graceful. You could even say they were dance like. You could even say they were beautiful. He was not as large and physically imposing as the other Titans but somehow I knew the female Titan Aurora would prefer this one above all the others.

In front of the three wizards and the lineup of young Titan warriors I inscribed the double lines in the dry sand, recreated the concentric hemispheric transport dome and the Titan and I evaporated and returned to the future.

Where ? Tokyo, Japan.

Where does one begin? Where does one end? What does one share? What does one secret away?

The Source insisted that I pursue the creation of a pattern, which is basically the mold for the creation of something, the creation of something new. I knew from the 'get go' that the Source would not tell me how to accomplish this task but he would make it possible for me to somehow succeed at this challenge. Initially I thought sharing the details of this process completely was important. But, subsequently I changed my mind and decided that these things, though available to all, should be shared by me, with none.

I did eventually figure out a way to create the pattern or mold if you prefer. I also found a way to power it up and initiate the process of creation and engaged the engine that creates all physicality. Now I must wait and see if my creation becomes a reality and then decide what to do with it. It's funny how, "The closer your destination, the more you're slip sliding away."

The key to accomplishing this un-imaginable task was to engage the "Buddha of the cave" by traveling back through time. We had long conversations and even though it was a challenge for me to grasp the reality of what I encountered there, it was key to accomplishing this seemingly impossible task in just three days.

As it turned out, we were in Japan during this process. Even though the Japanese are secular in their daily lives, culturally they have been steeped in Shinto and Buddhist philosophy. This is evident in every aspect of their lives. This certainly facilitated in the fulfillment of this particular challenge.

Inside the cave where I located the Buddha there was almost nothing. The opening to the cave was small, about two and a half feet wide and maybe five feet high. The floor of the cave sloped upward ending twenty-five or thirty feet into the side of the mountain. At the very end of the cave the Buddha sat inside of a hollowed out spherical alcove a couple of feet above the floor of the cave. It was no more than four feet in diameter. The cave itself at this point was about eight feet high and maybe eight feet wide. Directly in front of the Buddha was a conical shaped fire pit comprised of oval shaped stones all approximately five or six inches in diameter stacked on top of each other forming a truncated cone. The base was about two and a half feet in diameter and the top of the cone had an opening about three or four inches in diameter. In the side of the cone facing the Buddha there was an opening to put twigs or small sticks of wood into. There was no mortar to hold the stones together so flames from the small fire were visible inside the stacked stones. This obviously provided adequate warmth reflected back from the conical enclosure in which sat the Buddha. Outside the cave, which was located in what was at the time probably Tibet, the temperature was extremely cold but inside where the Buddha sat was comfortably warm. On his right side there was a small bundle of sticks and on his left side there was a small metal plate with a few small biscuit like breads. The fireplace provided warmth and subdued lighting.

The cave itself was far up on the side of a mountain with no trail or visible way for anyone to get there. Besides the mountain was covered in ice and snow. I asked the Buddha how he managed. He offered me a small biscuit and as he removed it form the plate it was instantly replaced with another biscuit. The biscuit was plain tasting and crunchy like hardtack. He then handed me a stick from his small stash. It looked and felt like wood but it had no growth rings and was quite lite.

He told me that the sticks would burn for fifteen or twenty minutes each. They gave off a great deal of light and heat but they were smokeless and like the hard little biscuits, they replenished themselves. He added that the wood left no ash and the biscuits provided nourishment with no residue, meaning he never had to go outside to go to the bathroom. I told the Buddha that I had never seen anything like the sticks or the biscuits. He said that was because he created them out of nothing. He then produced the molds for each and showed me how they worked.

Taka Matsu

Taka Matsu in Japanese translates roughly as big tree. While we were in Japan we stayed in a traditional Japanese home in Kyoto. This small two story dwelling of approximately 800 square feet was several hundred years old. We were asked by its owners to be very quiet, so that we would not disturb any of the neighbors. We all slept on the floor on traditional straw matts. My neck was killing me from carrying a backpack all day. I woke up at five o'clock in the morning local time and my neck was much worse. I knew I was going to be in for a very long day with a bad stiff neck.

Noki Matsu & the three Spirits

Noki Matsu translates roughly as pine tree in Japanese.

I posed these questions for myself to ponder:
Why was it necessary to be so quiet?
And, were there any spirits it this old house?

Three different faces appeared before me. Each one of the faces was in its separate, oval antique frame. The three faces were all old and wrinkled so I wasn't sure if they belonged to males or females. My guess was that the top two were of men and the bottom one probably was of a woman.

The name of the man in the top picture was O-Ji-San.

The name of the man in the middle picture was Suji-Wan.

The name of the woman in the bottom picture was Nagori.

O-Ji-San was a prior owner that died in the house.

Suji-Wan was a later owner who also died in the house.

Nagori was a renter who also died while living in the house.

All three of their spirits were sleeping in the house. Noki-Matsu, the spirit of the house itself was also asleep. That was the real reason for the admonition, not to make noise so as to not awaken or disturb the sleeping spirits. The question for us was how to do that, with my five-year-old granddaughter jumping around and yelling all the time.

I told an old Japanese joke in which I complained loudly that my neck was killing me, which it was, that my back was broken and my right foot was falling off. Laughter erupted from all who had ever visited in this house in the past, waking all three sleeping spirits of the dead people as well as the spirit of the house itself, which was constructed from logs of pine trees with pine wood flooring and a pine tree limb railing for the stairs.

I was told that anyone who stayed in this house and offered a small bowl of rice would have their pains in their back or neck or foot relieved.

I went back to sleep and when I awoke the pain in my neck was gone.

Tsubomi Nagori

In Japanese this translates as flower bud or blossom.

Last night I was talking with the spirits that I had awakened by shouting a saying in Japanese that translates as, "My neck was killing me, my back was broken and my right foot was falling off." Laughter erupted from all of the people who had ever visited this small house. I wanted to know more about each of the four spirits.

The first spirit I talked with was Oji-Wan. He owned the house long ago. He lived and died in the house. But, because he had no son to inherit the house, his spirit remained in the house to watch over it.

The second spirit I talked with was Suji-Wan. He was another man who subsequently lived in this same house and also died there. He too never had a son to inherit the house so his spirit also remained in the house to watch over it.

The third spirit turned out to be a female. She was the daughter of Suji-Wan. Her name was Nagori. She never married but lived and died in her father's house. I told each of these three spirits that I would take them anywhere they wanted to go if they decided to leave this old house.

The fourth spirit turned out to be Noki-Matsu, the spirit of the house itself. I also offered to take Noki-Matsu anywhere it wished to go. Then I went to sleep. I woke up later in the middle of a lucid dream. I found myself with this diminutive young girl who appeared to be in her early twenty's. She looked like a Native American to me. When I talked with her, she said that she wanted to stay there with me. We seemed to be some where in the countryside. When I told her that I was already married and that she needed to find some-one her own age that she could share her life with, she became very emotional and left crying.

Subsequently I put two and two together and re-alized that this young girl was actually the old lady Nagori when she was young. So, I summoned her back to where I was. That was when she confirmed that her name was Tsubomi which means flower bud or blos-som and that her other name was Nagori.

She was anxious to leave so I transported her to the 'Place of Re-assignment' where she was given another life. She re-incarnated but I have no details regarding where or when that was to be.

Oji-Wan

Last night I talked again with the first spirit, the old man Oji-Wan. I told him that the spirit of the old woman Flower Blossom was gone. She chose to have another life with the opportunity to have a family in another place and another time. I presented to Oji-wan the opportunity to have a son in another life and he accepted the chance and wanted that life to be at Mt. Fuji. We traveled together to the desert place of re-assignment where I explained to the Assignment Angel what Oji-Wan requested. She fumbled through her basketful of lives and presented Oji-wan with the scroll of his next life.

Next I presented the same opportunity to Suji–Wan after explaining that the old man and the old woman had both accepted the opportunity to have another life and were no longer in the house. He also accepted this opportunity to have another life with the chance to have a son. His request was different. Suji-Wan wanted to return to the past and become the son he never had. We ventured together to the place of re-assignment where I explained Suji-Wans' request to the Assignment Angel. She seemed un-fazed by his request, searched through her satchel of scrolls and presented his next life to him as the son he never had. That would make him the father and the son. I have no idea how that scenario played out in the past.

After that I was talking with the spirit of the house, Noki-Matsu, and asked what he would like to do now that the three other spirits were no longer in the house. I told him he could stay there in the house or go somewhere else or he could travel with me. When I first encountered the spirit of the house Noki-Matsu he appeared as this giant ugly demon but after I proposed some alternatives for him he appeared as a diminutive creature a little over three feet tall, perhaps thirty-eight to forty inches in height. He was chubby and covered all over with brown hair the color of tree-bark. He didn't appear threatening at all. While we were talking, my son, with whom we were traveling in Japan, became very ill. He became nauseous and began throwing up repeatedly. I asked Noki-Matsu if he knew of anyone who might be able to help my son with this affliction.

The house spirit took me to a small place where several people were in line to see an old lady who was offering remedies for various ailments. She appeared to be very old and looked quite ugly sitting there at her tiny little table located inside a tiny room from which she dispensed her potions. I pushed my way in and made it up to the front of the line.

With my wizard's powers of observation I could see that the old lady was actually death in disguise. So, I transformed myself into the Sapphire Wizard and whacked her with my wizard's magic staff. She disintegrated and a small ball of light floated up. I grabbed it and returned to the house in Kyoto where we were staying and administered it to my son. I also gave him some magic potion that I have that can cure any ailment and counteract any poison. My son stopped his vomiting immediately but it took many more hours before he was re-hydrated and feeling normal again.

After I determined that my son was going to survive I went back to the old lady's small house with Noki-Matsu, the pine tree spirit of the house and magically re-constituted the old lady from the pile of shards lying on the floor. She was now just a plain old lady, for Death had been vanquished yet again through the use of a wizard's powers. When Noki-Matsu witnessed this scenario, he told me that he too wanted to leave this ancient house in Kyoto Japan where he had resided for hundreds of years and travel with me wherever our adventures would take us.

Christmas Imp

This morning my dog came to my side of the bed and jumped up with his front paws on the bed at 2:00 a.m. He was not happy about something but he wasn't barking or whining. I looked all around but I didn't see anything but the hair was standing up on the back of my neck so I knew there had to be something there somewhere.

I went out to the front of the house and there sat the night bus waiting for me with the folding doors open. When I got inside of the bus I asked Brad, the bus driver, what he was hauling tonight. He said, "Christmas dead. They are the worst."

Today is the 30th of December so they must have been dead for a few days by now if they died on Christmas Day. Brad said that he was hauling the dead and dying from Christmas. He told me that with these troublemakers it had to be a two-step process with a way station in between. They were very unruly because they died or were dying on such a big holiday like Christmas.

It took jus a few minutes to get to the drop off destination. Brad said he would be back for them in a week or two after they had a chance to cool off. I was back home again in less than five minutes. Then, the fun began.

When I got back to the bedroom I gave the place a thorough going over. There was this skinny half transparent thing standing in one corner that looked to me like an imp. I asked what it was doing there. The imp said that it had hitched a ride on the back of the Night Bus. When the bus stopped in front of my house the imp got down from the back of the bus. I asked again what it was doing there in my bedroom. It said that it didn't know. I asked what it was doing riding on the back of a bus filled with dead people. He didn't know. I asked what his name was. He didn't know.

He didn't know what his name was. He didn't know where he had come from or where he was heading. He said that he never attended school and he was very ignorant. I finally asked if he were dead or alive. He didn't know the answer to that question either.

I am familiar with imps but this one was very different. No matter what questions I asked him his answer was always the same…that he didn't know. Because he appeared to be sort of there and sort of not there I thought perhaps he had become separated from his body that was possibly still alive but unconscious somewhere but he had no idea where that might be.

I enlisted the assistance of a departed corgi named Peaches that hung out around my house to help locate the imp's misplaced body. With the help of the corgi we were finally able to locate the imp's body. I told the imp to get back into his body and put it on like a wet suit. He finally got into the body but wouldn't quit talking. When he finally stopped complaining I was able to put a few drops of this magical elixir into his mouth that was supposed to counteract any poison and cure any ailment.

The Imp finally regained consciousness and began to move around. When he finally sat up he said he had the worst headache ever. I checked the back of his head and he had a child's tomahawk buried halfway into his head. Apparently some kid hit him on the head with his tomahawk. After I removed it the Imp said he felt much better.

I didn't know what to do with the Imp so I took him back to my house with the understanding that he was not to cause any trouble for anybody while he was there. Trouble is what Imps are known for. He was going to hang around in the back yard until I could figure out what to do with him.

Sixth Dimension

We live in a three dimensional world or so we believe. Some people are willing to expand that view to four, by calling time the fourth dimension. Apparently that view, though believed by most, is incorrect and short sighted. Last night I ventured into the sixth dimension. This is how that occurred.

At 2:00 o'clock in the morning I caught the Night Bus. When I boarded the bus I asked Brad, the bus driver, to take me to the Sixth Dimension. He then put the bus through several bizarre maneuvers. He spun the bus around its long axis then rolled it over a few times. It was actually three spins and three rolls then we stopped and I got off.

The first thing I did was to expand my point of view to include all four cardinal directions plus the above and the below simultaneously giving me the global spherical view. What happened next was the encroachment of a spherical inclusion-advancement coming from all four cardinal directions. This process continued until my perception was squeezed from four directions until it became straw-like in a vertical position. Around the base of this straw a doughnut shaped toroid began to form with the straw sticking up and out of the doughnut hole.

That my friends, is how my three dimensional mind perceives a six dimensional reality.

Monster Mash

A couple of days ago the Source told me that it was time for me to be exposed to the 'Monster Mash'. He didn't elaborate or explain any further as to what the Monster Mash was or how I should get there. He felt that I was ready now to go there on my own.

First I tried going on the 'Night Bus' but that didn't work out so well. The next night I tried taking the 'Night Train' and that didn't go so well either. Last night I tried again for the third time by first locating the doorway to 'Monster Mash.' Then, I proceeded to enter through the door marked 'Monster Mash'.

The door itself was not that unusual but it was actually thicker and heavier than an ordinary door. It was made of solid wood more than two inches thick. Most doors are less than two inches thick. The upper half had frosted glass in it but the glass itself was almost half an inch thick. The words, MONSTER MASH, were stenciled onto the thick security glass in large upper case black letters. The surface of the glass was not smooth but textured and bumpy. The door opened outward hung in a solid rock wall revealing a tunnel through solid stone with straight vertical walls, a flat floor and an arched ceiling. The tunnel was a little over seven feet long and seven feet wide. The highest point on the arch was a little less than eight feet. This tunnel opened into another world filled with all sorts of monsters of different sizes, shapes and colors. The monsters were all bipedal and reminiscent of dinosaurs that walked on two legs.

The monsters were all moving around aimlessly ignoring each other and me as well. In an effort to better understand what they were and what the point of me being there was, I first observed them through the rose colored glasses. That made them all more colorful. Then I looked at them through the double-lensed pince-nez spectacles. They then appeared to all be small rodent size monsters. With the reflection from the magic sword they all appeared as different colored monster mice. Finally with the use of the rose colored glasses along with the double-lensed pince-nez spectacles and the reflection from the sword of truth, they all appeared as small mice all wearing different colored clothing walking around upright on their hind legs.

None of this made any sense to me until I witnessed them interacting with each other. They were all small talking mice. They completely ignored each other unless they were interacting with another mouse attempting to get something from the other mouse. All of their interaction was through flattery and deceit.

Then I understood that 'Monster Mash' was an allegory of how we humans run around ignoring everyone else, unless we are trying to get something from them through our flattery and lies.

We are all monsters and our interactions with each other, is the, 'Monster Mash'.

When I discussed this with the Source he was

pleased that I understood what the lesson actually was. I asked him if I were still a wizardling or was I now a wizard. His only comment was, "You're getting there…you are getting there."

Take it to the Limit

Last night while I was walking with the Source he looked up at the sky and asked me what I saw up there. I didn't see anything, absolutely nothing. Then he looked down at the surface we were walking on and asked me what I saw down there. I didn't see anything, absolutely nothing. He asked me to look to my left and to my right and wanted to know what I saw there. My answers were the same, absolutely nothing. Then, he turned to me and said, "Take it to the limit. Give it your best effort."

I was completely baffled by his request. The first thing I did was to go to 'the place' to store up as much energy as I could because I had no idea what might transpire from this request.

I thought about catching the night plane that comes at 1:00 o'clock but decided that might not be such a great idea. The same thing happened when the night bus came by at 2:00 o'clock in the morning. It just didn't feel right. It didn't feel like that was what I should do.

Before the night train came by at 4:00 o'clock I got a few things together and went out to wait for the train to come by. When the conductor got down from the train and asked me where I wanted to go I told him I wanted to "Take it to the Limit." He told me to tell the engineer up in the cab and yelled as loud as he could, "All aboard." I was the only one standing there.

When I told the engineer what I wanted to do, he got up from his seat and turned the controls of the old steam engine over to me. I had no idea what I was doing and no idea what I should be doing. I know steam engines can actually run pretty fast depending on how much pressure you can get up in an old boiler like this engine had.

"Take it to the limit," what did that mean? I put the engine in reverse and backed it up slowly until the slack was taken out of the couples. They use to do that when I was a kid watching the steam engines come and go on the Southern Pacific Railroad. Then, I eased it forward so we didn't spin the drive wheels as the train started to move. It began slowly increasing speed. I checked the pressure gauge as the needle creped past 100 PSI. I thought I might end up blowing the boiler apart trying to take it to the limit. Then I asked myself the question, taking what to the limit? For me that was the real issue. Taking what to the limit? No one said I had to take this train to its maximum speed. That would surely end badly with a driver who didn't even know how to stop this thing. Instead I decided to take it to the limit in terms of maximum distance traveled with the existing load of coal in the coal car.

I got it up to twenty-eight miles per hour and kept

it there with the boiler pressure on the low end of the green scale on the pressure gauge. We ended up stopping for water several times but in the end we finally run out of steam when the coal ran out. We had made it all the way to the town of Show Low in the White Mountains. That was a real accomplishment, in and of itself.

When I saw the Source he told me that he was very surprised. He thought I would go for the maximum speed and the maximum boiler pressure and probably blow the boiler apart. He was surprised that instead I went for the distance. I took the distance to the limit instead. I had given it my best effort. I had been shrewd.

The Plunge

Late this morning at around 5:30 a.m., I was talking with the Source as we walked in the place of complete emptiness. He furrowed his brow, squinted, looked over towards me and said, "I think you are ready to take the plunge." I had no idea what he was referring to.

He asked me to look all around and tell him what I saw. I saw nothing in front of us, nothing behind us, nothing to our right, nothing to our left, nothing above us and nothing below us. There was nothing anywhere. He stopped and a verdant green valley appeared in front of us. It was bowl shaped surrounded by high mountains with a small stream traversing it from the right to the left. The whole scene was round and beautiful but surrounded by nothingness. As we stood on a ridge looking down at this idyllic scene he said that it was time for me to choose. Of course I wanted to know what he was talking about. My concept of 'taking the plunge' obviously needed some clarification.

"You have demonstrated the stupidity of a moron and the caution of an idiot. That scene before you is the world of the messenger. Once you enter into it you may never escape from it. It is your choice, to take that plunge or to not take that plunge. The task of a messenger is to deliver the message, no other. It is true you have been given the gift of a great seer and the gift of a great healer and the gift of time travel. These are all essential tools necessary to acquire a message but they are not in and of themselves the message."

True to form, I of course asked, "How do I enter?" He said to me, "Open your chest as though you were removing a sports coat" and I did. I found myself in the middle of this huge valley ringed by high mountains standing next to the burbling stream.

Ark

Late this morning, around 4:30 a.m., I was talking with the Source. He told me that he wanted to talk with me about the concept of ark. I of course mentioned Noah and his Ark and the Ark of the Covenant since those are arks that I am familiar with. He began his explanation with the two of them and then, moved on to expand his conversation to describe what an 'ark' is. He explained to me that an ark is essentially a safe place to store something of value.

So Noah's Ark was a place of safety from the flood for Noah, his family and many animals important to his locality and livelihood. The Ark of the Covenant was a place of safety to store and transport what is basically a contract between God and a nomadic tribe of people, the House of Israel.

The Source wanted me to become the Ark of Consciousness. He gave me the gift of awareness to share with others. He expanded upon this and said as a seer can see or a healer can heal, so to a dispenser of consciousness can make the blind man see or the deaf man hear for when you are awake your awareness sleeps and though your eyes are open you are blind and though you hear, your awareness is deaf and though you can speak, you say nothing.

So the Ark of Consciousness is the place where awareness is safely stored. The Source once again reminded me that the children I treat daily are the ones who have taught me how to shift my awareness and how to move consciousness from one place to another. They would help me to master this, the gift of consciousness, which was freely given and should therefore be freely shared.

A Time to Choose

Last night the Source asked me to walk with him. It was apparent that he was uncertain as how best to present the next challenge he had in store for me. He furrowed his brow and asked me to tell him what I saw to my left, to my right and straight-ahead in front of me. I looked all around and saw nothing, only blackness in every direction. He frowned and said, "You must choose a direction in which to travel. You may turn left or right or go straight ahead. There is no turning back." I saw only blackness in every direction.

The Source added, "If you go forward straight ahead, death awaits you. If you turn to the right, death is waiting for you. If you turn to the left, you will surely die." That all sounded really great. But, I still needed to choose from one of those three directions.

Since it always appears easier to continue going straight ahead in the direction that you are currently moving rather than turning abruptly to the left or to the right, I tried to discern what lay directly in front of me first. I projected my awareness out into the darkness as far as possible. This is what I saw: There was a thin young blond woman standing alone facing me. When I observed her through the rose-colored glasses she appeared to be poorly dressed and dirty with disheveled hair. When I used the double-lensed pince-nez spectacles she appeared emaciated wearing tattered rags. With the reflection from the sword of truth she was a skeleton. When I used the wizard's powers of perception she became a miniature 'Grim Reaper'.

Next I turned and faced to the right projecting my awareness as far as possible out into the darkness. What I saw was an African American female standing alone facing me. With the rose colored glasses she appeared to be poorly dressed with ratty hair. With the double-lensed pince-nez spectacles, she too became emaciated and dressed in rags. And, with the reflection from the sword of truth she became a skeleton. With the powers of observation of a wizard she too became a 'Grim Reaper'.

Then, I turned around and faced the other direction. There I saw a large rectangular window encased in its wooden frame. When I observed the framed window through the rose colored glasses, it was transformed into a large sliding glass patio door. With the double-lensed pince-nez spectacles, the door was open and with the reflection from the sword of truth, the figure of the 'Thinker' appeared seated on his rock in silhouette facing straight ahead instead of looking at me. With the power of the wizard's perception I became the 'Thinker' and an open door into the 'corridor' appeared.

Since I have previously entered the first two doors on the right side of the corridor and the first two doors on the left side, I chose to enter the third doorway on the right side of the corridor. As I entered it became the beautiful 'Secret Garden' I have visited many times before, first as a small child then later as a middle school child and now once again as a young man. This same young blond lady met me and extended her hand to me. We held hands and walked together into the lush green garden as it engulfed us. I asked what her name was and she replied, "Robin". I knew then that this was the direction I would choose. I told the Source that I had chosen to turn left. He vanished leaving me alone to ponder upon my future.

Spanish Crow

Last month on the night of the full moon, several crows finally arrived but they came empty handed. They all told me that they would no longer be coming with each full moon and they would no longer bring gifts for me. The justification that they gave to me was that now I was no longer a sorcerer and therefore they could no longer associate with me. They told me that I was evolving, that I was becoming a wizard and sorcerers do not have anything to do with wizards. I did the best I could to convince them that maintaining a working relationship with them could be mutually beneficial but their murder of magical crows would have no affiliation with a wizard even if in the past I had been voted King of the Crows, in essence King of sorcerers. They scattered into the night sky, never to return again.

Last night was the next full moon. It came on the tenth of February. I went out to the back yard a little after twelve thirty at night when I woke up. I sat down on the brick pavers and waited. After about fifteen minutes a single small crow landed on the fat middle fiber optic cable strung along the telephone poles behind our house. The crow just sat there unmoving. It looked like that was the only crow that had come and the only one that was coming. I sensed that this solo crow had no intention of coming down from the wires so, I transformed into a crow myself and flew up and landed next to the small crow on the wire and waited. The crow then flew down and landed in darkness behind the Valencia orange tree next to the wishing well. I followed and landed on the grass near the grapefruit tree. Out of the darkness emerged a tall thin female dressed in a black floor length evening gown. With her long jet-black hair, her high cheekbones and chiseled features she revealed her Spanish heritage. I knew her well. She lived in what is now Normandy in northern France. She came from time in the seventeen hundreds and lived alone in an elegant two story stucco house. She was a consummate shape shifter. She took my hand and we entered a portal that opened into her living room where she transformed herself into the old woman that she pretended was her mother. Without saying a word she transformed into a dog. I transformed myself into an eagle. She transformed herself into a solid black leopard. I transformed myself into a large lion. She stared at me. Then, I transformed myself into a wizard, the Sapphire Blue Wizard. Then I appeared as two wizards located in two different places at the same time. Then I transformed myself into three wizards. Then I became a giant salmon colored Cyclops with a huge club in my right hand dragging it on the floor.

She transformed herself back into that tall lovely Spanish lady and I transformed into myself and we embraced and danced slowly to the silent classical music emanating from inside our heads. She realized that having such a magnificent shape shifter like me, for a friend, was a gift indeed.

Princess of the Pale

Early this morning sometime after midnight the Source said to me, "Michael, walk with me." As we walked he held his hands clasped behind his back looking down as though in deep thought. I followed his lead and put my hands behind my back and looked down glancing occasionally at him from the side. After a few moments he said, "It is time for you to see the pale." I responded, "Like beyond the pale?"

In front of us appeared this shear fabric curtain, which was obviously the "Pale". He stood in front of the pale for a moment then in what looked to me like a quick karate move he whirled on his left heel and ripped open a big hole in the pale with his right hand that appeared to me to have been a large claw of some kind that was over two feet in length. We walked through the hole in the pale and he asked me to tell him what I saw.

I saw only blackness and nothing else. He said that this was the realm of the dead and it was separated from the world of the living by the pale. At that moment a young blond women who resembled 'Lady Gaga' flew by. She was wearing a shimmering transparent costume. She spun around in front of me and then she was gone. I asked the Source if she were Lady Gaga. The Source said, as he stooped down and picked up the sheer garment that she was wearing from the floor, "She was the Princess of the Pale." She had left that piece of the pale he had torn from the fabric of the curtain, which separated the living from the dead. He said that I was to close the opening he had made in the pale with that missing piece of fabric. Otherwise, the dead could come into the world of the living not as ghosts but as living dead. I said, "Like the Zombie apocalypse?" His response was, "No, not zombies... living dead. You may enter the world of the dead through this opening but you must always replace the torn fabric to keep the dead from returning to the world of the living."

When I got up this morning to go to the bathroom I stepped on a pile of sheer fabric that came from the pale. I had forgotten to cover the opening last night when we left the world of the dead. I hastily returned to that spot and replaced the missing fabric, hoping that not too many of the living dead had made their way back into our world, the world of the living.

Milk & Honey

The other night the Source turned to me and said, "Michael, walk with me." We walked together for a ways in silence before finally stopping. The Source asked me to tell him what I saw. We were standing in an area of rolling hills covered in tall golden grasses. There were no trees or bushes or roads or telephone poles or houses or farms or any animals to be seen.

The Source asked me what I thought this place was. The grass was tall and beautiful but not like prairie grass. Besides, there were too many rolling hills for us to be in the mid-west. I told him I thought we might be somewhere in Oklahoma or Arkansas but there weren't any trees or brush and there were no rocky outcroppings.

He told me that this was the land of Milk and Honey. This was the Promised Land, my Promised Land. I asked if this is where I would end up when I died. He said, "No" this is where I would live someday but he didn't say where it was. A small house with a peaked roof appeared on the top of a hill nearby and down in the valley trees appeared, seeming to line the edges of a small stream that wandered off and disappeared into the distance. The trees were all deciduous, no pine trees.

I made my way up to the house and found myself in a small kitchen where a table with two chairs was situated against one wall that was covered in old fashion wallpaper. There was a small refrigerator next to a small sink situated next to a four-burner stove. On the floor lay a Golden Retriever. I bent down, patted him on the head and scratched behind his ears. He was old like me; maybe there were just the two of us now.

I passed through the hall and out onto the front porch. There was a narrow walk winding up to the steps from a non-existent road. Next to the walkway there was a sign the size of a for sale sign, which read, "MINISTER of PERCEPTION". I guess that is my destiny.

Ancient Mariner

Last night my son who lives in Orange County called and said that there was something in his house causing problems and he wanted me to come over and get rid of it. I asked if he had any idea where it was or what it looked like. He couldn't provide me with any information other than it seemed to be draining his energy. I told him that I would be over sometime shortly after midnight but I wasn't sure exactly when that would be.

The first thing I did was to confer with the Facilitator. I was surprised when he volunteered to participate in this adventure. He even suggested the actual makeup of the team. It consisted of Sabatini the traveler's Buddha, Lucky the six year-old boy, the Wizard's Giant, the Wizard's Elf, the Facilitator and myself as the

Sapphire Blue Wizard. We assembled in my back yard and transported over together through a large portal, directly into my son's driveway in front of his house.

The Giant covered the front of the house. The Facilitator covered the back of the house. Sabatini and Lucky covered the pool house and the elf and I split up to check out the perimeter of the house and yard. The Elf went to the right and I went to the left. He made a complete circle on the right side of the house and I made a complete circle on the left side of the house, meeting back in front of the garage.

Sabatini and Lucky went through the pool house. The Elf checked out the crawl spaces under the house and I went through the attic spaces above the house. We systematically went through every room and every closet. Finally I found a character scrunched up hiding under the desk in the office. He looked like a gargoyle because of the way he was all scrunched up but you could tell that he was actually a person but very emaciated, old and wrinkled. Then began the inquiry into who and what he was and why he was there in my son's house.

I pulled him out from under the desk where the desk-chair should have been but he remained all scrunched up squatting on the floor gargoyle-like until I began dropping these small golden spheres about the size of ping pong balls one by one above him. I had no idea where they were coming from. They were materializing one by one in my hand and as I dropped them this character gobbled them up. With each ball he gobbled up he began to unravel and fill out. This process continued until I had dropped twenty-seven golden orbs. By then he was almost six and a half feet tall, very weathered with long straggly hair.

After much discussion with him I learned that he was the embodiment of all the sailors that dared challenge the angry seas in ancient times. He is known as the 'Ancient Mariner.' He told me that these golden spheres were what sustained him and that the oracle had told him that they could be obtained at my son's house. Where and how these magical golden spheres appeared in my hand, I have no idea. I stuffed this guy into the leather sack that I carry and then continued with my search of the rest of the house.

In the family room I found this really big blond haired guy with a crew cut sprawled on the sofa. He turned out to be the 'Lounging Lout.' I dispatched him as quickly as possible and we left my son's house. I assumed that the job had been successfully completed.

Blue Star

When I talked to my son the next day, he told me that things had gotten even worse so I would need to come back again that night to see what else was going on.

This time when I consulted with the Facilitator, before I ventured over to Orange County again, he suggested that I go alone but as a pinpoint awareness so that whatever was there would not know of my presence. I took his advice and went back over, even though it was earlier than normal for me at around ten-thirty that night. This time, since I didn't transport by portal but approached the house from above as pure awareness, I noticed what appeared to be a lot of dimly lit tiny blue lights in various areas on top of their clay tile roof. To get a better view of the roof I moved up higher and higher until my field of vision expanded to encompass the entire property. From that vantage point I could clearly make out the shape of a giant transparent starfish with blue organelles dotted throughout. This thing was so big that the ends of its five arms drooped down over the sides of the house. I had no idea what this thing was or where it had come from, what it could do or for that matter how I could get rid of it, so I returned to Tucson to give it some serious thought.

Since I was at a total loss I tried to connect the dots. All of these scenarios I encounter consistently contain two elements. One is a challenge and the other is the solution to the challenge. The challenge was always to identify the problem first and secondly to neutralize or eliminate the perceived problem. The Lazy Lout may have had something to do with the problem but the Ancient Mariner probably did have something to do with the giant starfish since they appeared at the same time.

Assuming that the Mariner may have brought the starfish with him I summoned the Ancient Mariner and transported back over to my son's house with him to see if he could help resolve this problem. Quick as the wink of an eye the Ancient Mariner removed the Giant Blue Starfish and they both disappeared in a flash. It's funny how things can happen like that.

Dead Man?

Monday a little after 5:30 in the afternoon my son called from California and told me I needed to come over and take care of a problem there at his house. I asked what the problem was and he said that there was a dead man staring into the window of the TV room at his house, which is on the second story. I told him I would be over later in the evening but probably not until after midnight to see what I could do about the problem.

I assembled a group of six to accompany me on this project. After we arrived I positioned different team members in specific locations to make sure all of the entrances to the house were covered before I went looking for the 'dead man'. It didn't take me long to find him. In no time at all I was engaged in a death struggle with this 'psycho'. His eyes were wild and he was trying to do me in. I kept asking him who he was, why he was there at my son's house, what he wanted, how he got there over and over again but he was not responding to my questions, only trying to kill me. I took out the 'sword of truth,' which can terminate anything living or dead and stuck the point under his chin. It didn't phase him that he was about to be terminated. That's when I knew that he was totally insane. As I struggled with this lunatic, I remembered the gift I had been given by the Source, which transforms a crazy person into a sane person with its application but the person has to be totally insane and completely disconnected from reality in order for it to be effective.

With its application this 'psycho' settled down and after awhile began to show signs of sanity. He finally told me that his name was Ralph but he still didn't know how he ended up at my son's house or why he was there. Ralph told me that he was born in Oceanside on August 17th 1942. That was about all of the useful information that he could provide. I didn't know if he was dead or not because I was dealing with his spirit. My son said that this guy was dead but there was no way for me to know that for certain. One thing for sure was that Ralph was not all there. I told him to settle down and take it easy and I would return later after I had given his situation more thought.

I asked several of my associates how I could determine if Ralph were dead or not but they didn't know how I would be able to determine that for sure. After a couple of hours I returned to where Ralph was. I found him sitting at a table outside of a sidewalk café in Tustin. We talked for a while but I was unable to get much more information out of him. I left him sitting there at the closed café and told him to stay put until I returned. I was really at a loss as to how I could determine for sure that Ralph was actually dead. I needed that information before I could determine what the next step should be. I finally broke down and consulted the Source. He usually is only willing to give me hints but this time he provided me with a specific solution.

The Source told me that it was impossible for me to know if a person were dead or alive by dealing with their spirit. He said that I needed to find Ralph's body and if his body was dead then Ralph was dead because a spirit never dies. It is eternal. Armed with this information I returned to where Ralph was waiting for me and we went in search of his body. We found it in the hospital. Ralph was unconscious or in a coma. I took him by the hand and got him back into his body. He started moving and began talking to family members there in the hospital. That was a little after two o'clock Tuesday morning. I assumed that Ralph might have followed my son home from the hospital where he does his surgery cases.

Ralph wasn't a dead man after all. He was the wandering spirit of a comatose man.

Joseph

The golden gondola comes by my house every morning at 3:00 o'clock. This morning I was involved in some other activities and didn't make it out to the place where the canal was until 3:18 a.m. We had a cold spell here and the temperature was down to 40 degrees. Maria, the gondola girl was not dressed properly to be outside in the cold waiting for me to arrive. I apologized for being late and took off my jacket and wrapped it around her shoulders and snugged it up because she was shivering and her teeth were chattering. Our conversation usually focuses on extraneous topics and activities and rarely involves the mundane and private personal accounts of what she does to occupy herself in my absence. With her being half frozen I engaged her in trivial conversation to distract her from the cold. I asked what she did today before I arrived.

Maria said she had done some embroidery work and read a story from the Bible. I asked her what the story was about. She told me that it was about Joseph. I assumed that perhaps she was referring to Joseph and his coat of many colors but she said that it was the story of Joseph and of his wife Mary and the birth of their son in a stable because there were no rooms available at the Inn where they had gone to pay their taxes in Bethlehem.

By the time we arrived at our destination on the other side of the canal Maria was no longer shivering and we disembarked and resumed our customary activities.

Subsequently I was talking with the Source and shared with him my conversation with Maria. He said, "Jesus was a good man, very talented." He then shared with me his perspective on reality. He said, "Sorcerers spend their lives seeking the 'Source' but few of them ever accomplish that objective. They use the dreamscape in their attempt to alter physical reality. On the other hand, wizards attempt to alter physical reality by dreaming up the dreamer and then altering the dreamer's dreams, emulating the machinery of creation. That is something that a sorcerer could never do. Ordinary men attempt to control their physical world by manipulating each other through religion and politics or fear and punishment. All religions promise eternal life as reward but eternal life is your birthright. Each of you will be born again and again and again and so too Buddha and so too Jesus."

The Unmasking

This morning a few minutes before 4:00 o'clock I went out to catch the Night Train, which comes by at 4:00 o'clock sharp. I haven't caught the Night Train for many months because I have been occupied with other activities. Normally the street is replaced with a rail bed of black ballast stone and a set of railroad tracks. The antique steam locomotive comes soon after and the conductor gets down out of the first car and ushers would be riders into the train.

This morning things were very different. Instead of the road bed there was a three dimensional geometric matrix of square cubes made up of iridescent tubes about eighteen to twenty inches square. These tubes were made up of dashes of light moving synchronously in clockwise motion. Here and there small pieces of what the scene normally looked like were evident. The train stopped and the conductor disembarked. The conductor as well as the train itself was largely comprised of smaller iridescent squares that were about half the size of the larger squares. They too were made up of tubes of moving dashes of light. I got on board and everything inside the train, including all of the passengers, were also made up largely of these same squares with intermittent patches of normal appearing structure. This was obviously not a train I was going to ride on.

I immediately left the train and engaged the Source in conversation about what I had encountered. The Source told me that because I was transforming into a wizard and was no longer a sorcerer, I was able to see more clearly the true nature of reality. The only thing that appeared as it normally would was the Source himself. I myself appeared as this same patchwork of squares with pieces of clothing and skin here and there. He said that I perceived reality as it actually is. All of what we think of as physical reality is merely an illusion. When I asked the Source why he appeared so normal and so complete and everything else seemed to be like a matrix or scaffold.

He said that this matrix is the scaffold upon which our physical reality is created and sustained and that the matrix itself is time. He said that in reality nothing physical actually exists. It is merely an illusion. He himself in reality is the only thing that exists. Everything else is illusion. When you unmask the matrix and remove time everything else vanishes and only he remains. Time is the Ticker, the Tocker, the Maker, the Taker.

Derelicts' Dump

I was awake this morning at 2:00 o'clock so I decided to check on Brad the raccoon driver of the Night Bus. When I got out to the street in front of my house the Night Bus was waiting for me with its doors swung wide open. I climbed on board, up the three steps and asked Brad how he was doing since it had been many months since I hitched a ride on his Night Bus. I didn't even bother to look back to see who or what Brad was carrying tonight. I just asked what he was hauling on this trip. He told me that he was hauling a load of derelicts to the dump.

I asked him what exactly he considered to be a derelict. Not strictly speaking a definition but what it took for someone to be considered as a derelict and be hauled to the dump. Brad the raccoon said anyone who didn't make a positive contribution to others or to the world in general, someone who refused to take personal responsibility for their own actions, someone who didn't respect themselves or others, someone who couldn't tell the truth, anyone who abused drugs or alcohol, someone with no redeeming qualities. At that point I turned around to see who was actually being hauled to the dump. There were men and women and even children. They did in fact appear to be a motley group. I even recognized some of the derelicts riding on the Night Bus heading for the dump. Some of them were still living so I asked Brad about that. He said that these derelicts were made up of the dead and dying as well as some not yet dead.

Before long, we arrived at Derelict's Dump. It was encircled with a chain-link fence that was ten feet high. The bus rose up into the air on scissor-like tall extensions and the back of the bus tilted backward like a dumptruck and all of the riders tumbled out on the other side of the fence into 'Derelicts' Dump'.

I asked Brad what would happen to them now. He said they would be slowly melted away by bubbling acid and sink into the dirt there in Derelicts' Dump.

Sutter's Mill

Sutter's Mill was the sawmill owned by John Sutter in 1850 where gold was first discovered. The mill was located on the bank of the American River in Coloma, California by a carpenter whose name was James Wilson Marshall. This set off the 'California Gold Rush'.

Yesterday my son called from Orange County, California and told me that his wife had just returned home from a yard sale where the personal possessions of a woman who had been killed there in that house were for sale. He insisted that I come over to his house and make sure that no spirits had accompanied her when she returned home.

I checked with the Facilitator for any specific recommendations that he might have regarding the makeup of the group going over to my son's house. He felt that I should go over as the Sapphire Wizard and take the Wizard's Giant and the Wizard's Elf along with me.

It was after one o'clock in the morning before we finally made it over there. The Giant covered the front of the house. The Elf covered the back of the house as I systematically went through the whole house room by room.

In the living room of his house I located a tall dark haired lady who informed me that her name was Shelly and that she was the woman who had died in the house where her personal belongings had been sold at a yard sale. I told her that she couldn't stay there at my son's house but I would be happy to take her anywhere she wanted to go. Shelly told me that she wanted to go to the California Gold Rush so I took her to Sutter's Mill in the year 1850. I asked her if she was going to be OK there by herself and she said that she would be just fine.

I returned to my son's house and continued my search. Where she had been there was some kind of disturbance. It was circular and about six or seven feet in diameter. It was obviously some type of disruption of the time space continuum. I knew that I would have to get that disturbance out of my son's house or it would cause trouble for him and his family. I rounded it up and stuffed it into a bag and left it at Sutter's Mill in the year 1850 where I had just left Shelly.

I continued my search through the rest of his house and located some kind of creature darting all around in my granddaughter's bedroom. I'm not sure exactly what it was but I stuffed it into a bag also and took it over to Sutter's Mill because I didn't know what else to do with it.

John Sutter the owner of the Mill and the carpenter James Wilson Marshall who discovered gold on the American River never got anything from their discovery. Shelly in the end may fair no better but I wish her well all the same.

Wizard's Bridge

Last week the Source asked me to walk with him. As we walked along everything grew darker and darker until we were in total blackness. Out of the darkness ahead of us a bridge appeared. It was an arched bridge sitting in the middle of blackness. We walked together across the wooden bridge. It was about thirty feet in length and five or six feet wide. There was nothing on either side of the bridge.

The Source turned to me and asked me to tell him what I saw when we reached the other side. I saw nothing. Everything was a medium gray. There was only grayness and nothing else.

The Source told me that we had just crossed over

the 'Wizard's Bridge'. The other end of the bridge began at the edge of the precipice. This end of the bridge ended at the place of infinite possibilities. Here there was nothing of substance everything was pure imagination. This was the world of the wizard where there was infinite potential and there was infinite possibility. Only a wizard could cross this bridge. This was where wizards created reality with their imaginings. He said I was no longer a wizardling but I was now a novice wizard.

Swimming Man

Last night I went to where the Facilitator and Lucky the six year-old child as well as Sabatini, the traveler's Buddha were sitting on a park-bench looking out on the event horizon and joined them by sitting down between the Facilitator and Lucky. I noticed a disturbance far out on the horizon and asked the Facilitator if he could see the disturbance. He said that he could see something far out at the edge of the event horizon but he had no idea what it could be.

I asked Lucky if he saw anything and he said that he didn't see anything. Then I asked Sabatini if he could see anything. He also said that he didn't see anything.

I turned to the Facilitator and told him that it was a man swimming, a man swimming steadily but not swimming towards us nor swimming away from us but his orientation was sideways to us. I could see the man swimming with strong steady strokes. He was doing the Australian crawl but he was not making any headway. He was staying in one spot. With each stroke he turned his face down in the sea and took a deep breath of water. With his next stroke he rolled his face above the surface of the water and exhaled what looked like water that was filled with different kinds of things

I told the Facilitator that the man was 'Swimming Man' and that he was swimming through time but he was not being affected by time itself. He breathed it in and breathed it out again as he kept on swimming, swimming, swimming. With my wizard's powers of observation I could see Swimming Man up close. Swimming Man was myself. I was sitting on the park bench with the Facilitator and I was swimming, swimming, swimming through time. I was the disturbance and I was observing this disturbance, unaffected by time.

Que Sara, Sara

It has long been theorized that 'Worm Holes' in space could actually exist. Even though they have never been definitively discovered, there is scientific evidence that supports their existence and with better understanding of the underlying physics involved it might someday be possible to utilize them for enhanced communications or even transport over vast distances through space and time.

I have been working on an analogous process, which I refer to as 'Time Tunnels'. On the surface they may at first appear to be like worm holes but they involve a different process. The time tunnel actually connects two distinctly different times directly so that real time communications are established. The there and then is directly connected with the here and now such that the there and then is in the present moment and the here and now is also in the same present moment even though they are otherwise separated by vast periods of time.

I am currently in the process of connecting directly with several different characters in several distinctly different times and places. These characters all exist in different past times. Once these time tunnels are well established and better understood, the next logical step is to make a connection into the future. Ultimately that process may have to be initiated from the future back into the present moment.

One critical element is the acquisition of an exact address in space and time combined with a real living person whose correct name and actual location has been established with date, place and time-certain some-where and some-when in a future time and place. Perhaps then we will begin to understand and appreciate the process of 'Prophecy'.

"Que Sara, Sara." "What will be...will be."

Comfort Zone

Last night I was walking with the "Source." Of late he has clasped his arms behind his back apparently in deep thought as he is looking down at the area in front of where we are walking. He stopped and hesitated for a moment before he asked, "Michael, tell me what you see?"

I looked all around and told the Source that I didn't see anything. Then he wanted to know what I could hear. I of course didn't hear a thing but to be completely honest I told him the only thing I heard was a low background noise that I have been aware of for many years, what is often referred to as tinnitus. That just seems to come with age but I didn't think that was what he was asking me about.

He said that as one ages, the clarity of information perceived by your sensory organs deteriorates. That is just a reality of the human condition. He elaborated further, "When you are here in this place and see nothing, hear nothing, sense nothing, you are within your own comfort zone. That should be a sign for you to move along and challenge yourself. You can use that as an indicator that you are not learning, not acquiring new skills, not gaining ground and not making any progress. When you begin to see things, to hear things, to feel things in this place that is a sign that you are back on track. You must force yourself to press on. Time is not your ally. Time is not your friend. Time is the measure and the beat of all things. The challenge for you is to become master of 'Time' itself.

The object is not to be comfortable but to be uncomfortable, very uncomfortable. That is the only way you learn."

Iserable

This is a strange name but a name, none-the-less. I asked the Source last night what he thought I should concentrate on at this point in time. He thought for a moment then he said, "Iserable." I of course had no idea what he was talking about for that is a word I have never ever even heard before.

The Source told me that Iserable was in actuality an ancient curse and it was time for me to be able to break a curse not just protect a single individual from the effects of a curse. Breaking a curse, that is quite a different thing for sure. That means terminating, destroying, abolishing the whole thing in its entirety even from the moment of its inception. That means un-creating it, which might entail un-creating its creator before the curse itself was even created.

The first task was to locate the whereabouts of this curse that goes by the name 'Iserable'. That didn't take too long but I obviously have a lot more work to do because I need to know exactly what the curse does and how it does what it does as well as its time and place of origin, who created it and what method or methods were used to create it and whether it was created using 'deep magic' or incantations, potions or poisons. I need to know if there are any antidotes or other counter measures that are effective in ameliorating any unanticipated contact with this curse as I attempt to unravel this whole thing. I will also need to know who has been affected by this curse and what problems could arise when I reverse not only the effects but also its affects. This could end up altering the past and that would in turn alter the present and the future.

The Source felt that the ability to break a curse was an important skill for a wizard to have. Whenever the source presents a challenge for me to solve he always leaves clues hidden somewhere that help me to unravel the challenge. This curse seems to abound everywhere and not have a pinpoint of origin. The more I looked into this curse, the more prevalent it became. I finally concluded that it was not only widespread but almost universal among humans.

While focusing on the name itself 'iserable' I noticed that by simply adding a single letter to it the word became 'miserable' and in French it could become 'Les Miserables' the famous musical. The theme of which is how miserable the human condition can become. So, I concluded that the 'curse' that the Source wanted me to identify is actually the 'Human Condition' and the antidote for it is to be present in the moment knowing full well that everything is temporary and everything is transitory including ourselves and the purpose of life is to live and let live for the only thing that you or

I take with us when our life ends is the memories that you and I have accumulated.

Deep Blue Sea

Amy passed away two weeks ago. I think fifty-seven years old is too young to die. I went looking for her a couple of days later. I found her wandering along the side of a road in the middle of the night disoriented and very confused. I picked her up and took her home with me to give her a chance to recover. I asked Amy if she wanted to attend her own funeral on Saturday but advised her that everyone there would be immensely saddened and greatly depressed. She would be totally ignored by absolutely everyone. She decided that she would skip her own funeral.

I had not seen Amy for three days so I decided to check on her last night. I found her hanging from some strange looking transparent flesh-like tentacle wrapped around her wrists with her arms extended outward behind her back. She was dangling there suspended in mid-air. It looked to be horribly painful for her. The place had no floor and no walls. The fleshy tentacle just ended about fifteen feet above her head. I had no idea how she ended up in this situation but I knew that I had to do something to get her out of her current predicament.

I checked with the Facilitator, and then with Sabatini, the Traveler's Buddha. Neither of them had ever seen anything like this before and had no idea how to remedy the situation. I knew I would have to go to the big guns if I were going to deal with this situation successfully. I summoned Ganesh, the Elephant God and Hanuman, the Monkey God. One appeared on one side of Amy and the other appeared on her other side. They stared up at the end of the tentacle, which ended in the middle of nowhere. They didn't know what to do with the situation either.

Next I rose above the place where the tentacle abruptly ended and there was nothing so I summoned Shiva the God of destruction. He appeared but said that he didn't know what to do with the situation. I summoned Krishna. He appeared and explained to me that this was a trap set for me by the devil. Amy was used as the bait to lure me there. If I cut the fleshy tentacle, which suspended Amy, the trap would be tripped and it would collapse in on me and crush my consciousness. If I left Amy there she would become increasingly angry and eventually she would be transformed into some sort of a demon from her unending pain and anguish. I had no idea what I could do to free Amy. I recalled a saying my mother used when she was in an untenable quandary when I was a little kid. I never really understood what it meant.

She would say, "Between the Devil and the deep blue sea." Since I needed to free Amy without cutting the dangling tentacle I summoned the Deep Blue Sea and it began pouring into the waiting trap. The clear cold water of the Deep Blue Sea revived Amy and floated her upwards freeing her entangled wrists. The tentacle shriveled up and disappeared when the pure cold seawater touched it. We were freed from the trap set for me by the Devil.

Now after all these years, I finally understand what my mother was trying to say when she would tell me that she was caught 'Between the Devil and the Deep Blue Sea.'

Chicago

No sooner had I rescued Amy than she told me she was going to catch the three o'clock to Chicago. I advised her to be careful. She said that she would be fine. Two days later I checked on her. I found her hanging from the ceiling with a heavy hemp rope tied around her wrists. Her back was covered with raised, red whelps. Someone or something had been beating her with a rope or whip.

I looked all around the dark dungeon and saw an ugly creature hunched in the corner still holding a long leather lash in his left hand. He looked like a gargoyle to me. I summoned Constantine from the distant past. He burst onto the scene and the gargoyle was swiftly decapitated. Once again I rescued Amy and brought her back to my house. I reminded her that there are a lot of really bad things a person can run into when they are no longer living but deceased. And, once again I offered to escort Amy to anywhere or any when that she wanted to go. But Amy has yet to make up her mind. So in the mean time I guess she will be hanging around my house.

I woke up and checked the clock. It showed 2:01 a.m. in large red numerals. I asked Amy if she wanted to go somewhere on the Night Bus. She said yes so we hurried out to the front of the house where the Night Bus stood waiting for us with its doors swung open wide. Brad asked her where she wanted to go. Amy said, "Take me home, I wanna go home."

Brad the raccoon bus driver took the first left and then another left. I assumed we were heading for her house located here in Tucson where she and her husband have raised their four daughters but I was mistaken.

We stopped somewhere in the distant past in an unknown place for me. When Amy stepped off of the bus she was a seven year-old little girl. She met her mom and dad there from fifty years ago. She introduced me to her family and told them I was 'Mikey'. I was a little kid just like her.

Amy said to me as she walked away together with her family, "Home is where your heart is" then, they all disappeared.

Two Gold Coins

I woke up a little after three in the morning. One

of our two Cardigan Welsh Corgis was panting. The air conditioner was on and the house was cool. There was no reason for the dog to be panting like she was. Over in the corner next to her dog bed there was a tall skinny man standing next to her. He was hunched over like he had a bad back. He was wearing tight pants that ended just below the knee. His leather shoes were black with a single buckle on them. His stockings were very dark in color. He wore a long sleeve shirt with a fancy collar and a dress coat with tails and open at the front. He moved towards me with his left hand extended. I had no idea as to who he might be or what he wanted from me.

I extended my left hand towards him with the palm facing upward. He placed two gold coins in my hand. I asked him what they were for. He said that one of the coins had the tails side facing upward and the other coin had the heads side facing up. That way I would always be prepared for whichever side landed up in a game of chance. I thanked him for the two gold coins and asked him who he was and what brought him to my bedroom in the middle of the night.

He told me that his name was Silverstein, Joseph Silverstein and he was from Vienna, Austria. He said that he was the same age that I was and he had come from the year 1703. When I asked him again why he had visited me, he said that he was a past incarnation of myself and he wanted me to be prepared for whatever chance brought my way. I thanked him once again and he disappeared.

About half an hour later I thought I should try to visit him in his year of 1703. When I arrived there where he was, he was in what we might call an alley. Three thugs were attempting to rob him at knifepoint. I transformed myself into a terrible beast and the three of them quickly fled as fast as they could. He was grateful for the rescue but wanted to know how I managed to pull off that transformation. I told him it was something that I learned along the way and I left it at that. I thanked him once again for the two gold coins. They may come in handy someday since life itself is really just a game of chance.

Animal Shelter

Last night while I was talking with the Source I asked him what activity I should concentrate on for the moment. The Source said that I needed to go and check on Amy. I assumed that I was finished with that project but I went looking for Amy as he suggested. I decided to take the Night Bus when it came by at 2:00 o'clock in the morning. When I got on board I asked Brad, the raccoon bus driver, what he was hauling tonight and he said, "Injured elephants". I looked around the bus and it was indeed filled with injured elephants. I told the bus driver that I needed a ride to wherever Amy was. He dropped me off after a few minutes ride.

I found myself in an animal shelter where every

kind of injured animal you could imagine were all around me with every injury they could possibly have sustained. Amy was standing at the far end of the treatment and recovery facility diligently treating all of these many sick and injured animals.

Apparently this was her calling. Apparently this was her heaven. This was where she wanted to spend her eternity helping these sick and injured animals to recover.

Memorial Day

It was 1:58 a.m. when I woke up on the morning of May 29th. I looked all around our bedroom and every thing appeared as normal but there was some sense of sadness present. I still had time to catch the Night Bus that comes by at 2:00 o'clock, so I rushed out into the street in front of our house. The Night Bus had not yet passed by.

When the bus stopped and opened the folding doors I jumped on board. Brad the bus driver looked at me and waited for me to tell him where I wanted to go. I had no idea where I needed to go so I said, "Take me someplace I need to go. Show me something I need to see." He closed the folding doors slowly, turned the bus around in the middle of the intersection and headed back up the same way he had just come. When we got to the 'T' at the end of our block he turned left instead of turning right the way he had arrived. We didn't go too far, maybe three or four blocks, before he stopped the bus, opened the door and waited silently for me to disembark. As I stepped onto the ground outside, the bus disappeared. Brad the bus driver never spoke a word to me the whole time.

It was almost dark but I couldn't tell if it were pre-dawn or dusk. I didn't know where I was. As I walked I could feel the crunch beneath my feet and hear the distinct sound my shoes made as I walked across volcanic sand and gravel. I was high up on the beach of a volcanic island. In front of me there were several young men sitting on jerry cans around a smoldering fire. There were no flames visible only the thick gray smoke billowing up from the coconut husks they were burning. They were all wearing wrinkled khaki pants. Some of them had sleeveless undershirts on; others were bare-chested with their dog tags hanging down from around their necks. Some of them were smoking cigarettes others were staring silently into the plume of smoke, which they hoped would keep mosquitos at bay. I asked the guy sitting on the jerry can closest to me what time of year it was. He replied curtly, "April of Forty-Five."

On the far side of the fire a young man took his harmonica out of his pocket and began to play a lively Irish tune in an effort to cheer up the 'boys' before a coming battle. When he finished he smacked his harmonica down on his leg hard several times to dry it out a bit before secreting it away in his back pocket. That was when I recognized him. He was my father. He was twenty-six years old and he was waiting there on the beach for the sun to rise somewhere in the Solomon Islands, in the Pacific Theater. I was two years old and safe back home.

Today was May 29th. It was Memorial Day, our National day of remembering those who have served in the armed forces. I remembered my father, just as he remembered the men of his crew who served with him in the United States Navy during World War II.

Gunnery Sargent

Last night at 10:45 p.m., I went looking for Andrea's Death. The objective of this project was to identify her death and attempt to enlist her death in the process of modifying her perspective. Since each of us have our own personal death that is ever close at hand, it wasn't that difficult for me to locate her death. The next step in this process was to gather as much information about her death as possible in an effort to determine what positive contribution her death might be able to provide for her.

At first her death was reluctant to provide me with any personal information. He finally said that his name was Blinn, which I thought was probably not true. Later he admitted to me that his real name was actually Blair and that he had been a Gunnery Sargent in the Marine Corp. Lying is unusual behavior for a dead person and that concerned me greatly as to his utility in this effort.

Eventually I uncovered the following personal information about Gunnery Sargent Blair. His mother was Jamaican and his father was an American Anglo. His father abandoned the family when he was young and his mother raised him and his younger brother alone. They were always on the verge of poverty. He married young and enlisted in the Marine Corp. He had two sons. His wife divorced him while he was deployed. He blamed his mother for the loss of his father and he blamed his ex-wife for the loss of his two sons. He was overly strict and overbearing and carried his grudge against women into his role as Andrea's death. He committed suicide at age thirty-five and that is how he wound up with this assignment, which he chose as opposed to spending one hundred years in purgatory for being a jerk and committing suicide.

After talking with him for a couple of hours I concluded that Gunnery Sargent Blair was the main source of Andrea's personality disorder and he would be unable or unwilling to facilitate in the process of altering her perception of herself and her relationship with the world itself.

I consulted with the Source and asked him if there were any way possible for Andrea to be assigned another personal death. The Source told me that I would have to take that up with the 'Reassignment Angel'. I of course had never even heard of such a thing. But, that didn't keep me from trying to locate them.

It actually was not that difficult. I located the 'Re-assignment Angel' in a place that reminded me of a convent. The Angel appeared to me as a Nun in her late fifties. She was dressed conservatively but was not wearing a habit and did not have her head covered. Her hair was silver-gray and on the short side. I was able to convince the Reassignment Angel to reassign Gunnery Sargent Blair and to give Andrea a new death but the angel said that this was highly irregular and I would be required to personally sign three copies of a multipage contract before she could allow this transfer to proceed.

I didn't take the time to read the contract before I signed all three copies in my own blood and I didn't bother to ask what would become of Gunnery Sargent Blair but I knew this was the only possible way for Andrea to have a chance to restore herself and her disintegrating family. It would have been nice to get a copy of that contract but I guess I'll just have to wing it.

Juniper

I went back the next night to check on Andrea's new Death. No death was there. But there was a skinny black demon that was almost six feet tall. I quickly dispatched the demon, no questions asked. I went back several times during the night to see if Andrea's new death had arrived but she was still alone so I decided I should wait there and keep an eye on her until her new death arrived. I discovered that she had a huge hole in her abdomen. That is a really dangerous condition and can lead to all sorts of very bad outcomes so, I patched her tummy up as well as I could and waited with her for her death to arrive.

A little more than twenty-four hours after the contract had been signed in triplicate Andrea's new death finally arrived and introduced herself to me as Juniper. She told me she had been very busy tying up loose ends before she could come. Juniper reminded me an awful lot of Mary Poppins. She was wearing a funny little hat and even carried an umbrella with the curved handle hanging down over her arm. I explained to Juniper that apparently Andrea's Death had become enamored with her and was jealous of her husband and wanted to keep Andrea all to himself. He was creating all kinds of problems between the two of them and that even extended to their two young children as well as creating problems with the rest of the extended family.

I told Juniper that she would need to concentrate all of her efforts on keeping the family intact and giving Andrea the chance to recover from the many years of abuse by her own personal death. I will be checking on Andrea often to see if she is making any progress.

Four-leaf clover

I was asked to look into a situation that had degenerated over time and has reached a critical state. My first response was to contact the Source. I asked the Source who would be the best person to query regarding the current situation. The Source said for me to ask the person at the heart of that situation and he emphasized that I should listen very carefully to his response. So, that is exactly what I did.

At 12:47 a.m., shortly after midnight I arrived at Phillip's home. When I encountered him he was extremely angry. I grabbed the wrist of his left arm and he strongly resisted my efforts. My first response was to share with him the 'Gift of love' for himself. For you must first learn to love yourself before you can love another. I had no idea what was causing all this anger so I placed a psychic bomb between the two of us and detonated it in case his anger was coming from a demon inside him.

The next thing I did was to transport the two of us into 'Dream Time' and when we arrived there we were met by Aru, the keeper of Dream Time. The three of us began our 'Walk About' in the outback of Australia in Dream Time. Phillip and I both appeared to be much younger and we were dressed in only a thong like Aru. He led the way carrying his spear. Phillip followed Aru and I ran behind to make sure that Phillip didn't get lost along the journey. We ran and ran and ran, barefoot as only an Aborigine can do, never stopping the whole day.

Finally we arrived at a crystal clear lake where a waterfall tumbled down into it from the cliffs high above. Phillip and I jumped into the clear cool water as Aru stood watch from above. We sank down to the bottom, which was maybe fifteen feet deep and there we met an identical twin of Phillip. The two of them embraced and held hands as we floated back up to the surface together.

I assumed that this other twin of Phillip must be a part of his total self that became lost and was separated during a near death experience in Phillip's past. Based on this assumption I rejoined the two halves and Phillip became the whole person that he had been before that near death experience. I thanked Aru for his wisdom and assistance in resolving this perplexing situation for Phillip. With that I returned Phillip to his home now once again a complete person. Then I returned home.

Shortly after that a Hispanic man, about five feet six or seven inches tall who appeared to be in his mid fifties with a neatly trimmed mustache and salt and pepper gray hair materialized in my bedroom and approached me extending his left hand. In his open palm he held a cloverleaf still on its stem and presented it to me. He said that he was Phillip's Father and he wanted to thank me for helping put his son back together. It was 1:08 a.m.

I went out to the 'Event Horizon' and sat down on the park bench between the Facilitator and the young boy Lucky and showed them the four-leaf clover. As Lucky picked it up and was admiring it, Sabatini, the Traveler's Buddha's saffron robe was transformed from a faded dusty old garment into a brand new saffron robe. We sat silently together on the park-bench staring out on the calm waters of the event horizon.

I personally recommend for Phillip to start doing Tai Chi. The slow Tai Chi should be done initially and then later possibly the martial arts style of Tai Chi. Any psychotropically active medications should be discontinued by decreasing the dose to one half for two weeks and then in the third week reduced by one half again for another two weeks and then discontinuing them entirely. A healthy diet and abstaining from alcohol, tobacco or any other drugs would be advisable.

Ligot

Ligot is a word I encountered a few days ago. I am not sure what it is exactly. I have a vague idea based on the context in which the word was used. I don't know if it is a thing or a concept or a belief or exactly what but I think it is worth the effort to try to find out. It occurred to me that whatever ligot turns out to be, it might possibly have some connection with the anger Phillip is struggling with.

I asked the Source if he would tell me anything about the term ligot even though I was quite sure that he wouldn't do so. Like usual I was going to be on my own in dealing with this challenge.

After many unsuccessful attempts to get at the meaning of the word ligot I decided to go to Vishnu's Island to see if anyone there could provide me with some insight. I situated myself in front of the fire pit with its smoldering embers. First I invited Hanuman the Monkey God to come to the fire pit, which was our usual gathering place. I asked Hanuman if he knew anything about ligot and then proceeded to describe it, as I understood its nature. Hanuman said that he had never heard of ligot and was adamant that a thing like that would be a warrior's greatest enemy for emotions could never be allowed to enter into mortal combat.

Next I invited Shiva the destroyer, the God of destruction to come. He arrived in short order but he too said that he had never heard of such a word. He stated that the goal of destroying anything was always in preparation for creating something new that would replace what has been destroyed. I knew that Ganesh worked in concert with Shiva to create the new to replace the old so it was unlikely that he would know anything that Shiva did not already know.

The next God I invited to come to the fire pit was Krishna. He always provides me with valuable insight into my inquiries. Krishna said that ligot was not a demon or a god but actually a state of mind that developed in the unsophisticated minds of jungle tribesmen when they were confronted with primal fear of the unknown and great loss because they lacked the coping strategies that better educated people have at their disposal. He suggested that I seek advice from the Buddha. So I did. When the Buddha arrived, he said to me, "You look familiar. I think our paths have crossed before." I told him that I was a traveler and that I have been in many different places at many different times. I asked him about the word ligot and asked what information he could give me concerning it.

The Buddha said, "Ligot is the response of uncontrollable rage that arises from within primitive minds of jungle tribesmen when they encounter a tragic loss combined with the extreme fear of the unknown. All human suffering has its origins in their attachments to things and their attachments to their beliefs, for nothing is permanent. All things pass away. True bliss lies in living in the moment for the past has gone and the future never comes. Only this moment is real. We will meet again when our paths cross." Then he was gone.

Welder

I thought that the Ligot inquiry might reveal an effective strategy for me in diminishing the anger management problems Phillip was experiencing but that did not appear to be the case so I decided to see if Phillip's own personal death might provide a viable alternative.

I found his death lounging in the living room with a welder's shield propped up on the top of his head. This is what I was able to discover about him. He was a welder but he had injured himself apparently in a fall and had been on disability for a long time. During this extended period of dependency he had grown bitter because he believed he was not getting enough financial support from the 'System'. He said that his name was Ralph and he was killed in some kind of freak accident when he was thirty-five years old. He was poorly dressed and unkempt, wearing jeans and an open blue work shirt with long sleeves over a soiled white undershirt. He needed a shave and was grumpy. I didn't buy the last name that he provided me with. I finally got out of him that he accepted this job of being Phillip's death in lieu of being sent to Purgatory to do some really unpleasant things for a period of some two hundred years.

The more I probed and questioned him about what he had done to end up in this situation, the more concerned I became about his capacity to encourage Phillip in any positive way. As I continued to grill him he grew younger and younger until he was regressing into his teen years. At one point he was sitting in a wheelchair unable to walk on his own. I pushed him back further into his past until he was younger still and before he ended up incapacitated in a wheelchair. At that point I took him outside the stream of time and moved forward many years before re-inserting him back into the stream of time. The results were quite amazing. By not allowing him to make those same poor choices the end results for him were very different. He was well dressed wearing a summer suit with a colorful tie and a white shirt. His suit was the color of coffee heavily laden with cream. He told me that his name was Raphael Cassini that he was a very successful businessman who lived in Italy. He had a beautiful family and a loving wife and two adoring children. He too died in a freak accident but his outlook on life and his appreciation for having lived were completely opposite, to that of Ralph the welder. By preventing Ralph from having the chance to make some really poor decisions, his life turned out totally different. Raphael would provide a positive influence in Phillip's life and remind him constantly of the value and importance of his family and the joy and pleasure they could bring to his life.

I was just getting settled back home in my bed when this decrepit old man with long white hair wobbled towards me. He clenched his walking cane tightly for support because he was drastically bent over at the waist. He said that he was Phillip's Grandfather and he had been hanging around since his parting because he was so concerned about Phillip. He thanked me for providing assistance in Phillip's hour of need. I asked him if he would like for me to help him get safely to wherever he wanted to go. He said he would appreciate any help he could get on his journey. I grabbed onto his left wrist so as not to loose him and we were off. We ended up in an area that had some scrub brush and deciduous desert trees outside of a small adobe house with a plank wood door. As Phillip's Grandfather pushed the door open he exclaimed, "Its just the way I remember it." A shaggy rust colored dog nosed her way between us and the grandfather, who by now was a young man. He said, "The dog she is still here, and there are chickens too," as he looked all around.

Later when I was visiting with the Source he turned to me and said, "I was very surprised at the way you managed that situation. That was very creative. I have never seen anything done quite like that before." I will take that as a compliment, which coming from the Source, is rare indeed.

Native American Proverb

Listen to the wind.
It talks.
Listen to the silence.
It speaks.
Listen to your heart.
It knows.

Luxury

I spent several hours on Wizard Island sitting under the pear tree as imaginings fell endlessly from its branches like snowflakes. When I awoke it was 3:32 a.m. I asked the question, "I wonder if anything comes by in front of the house at 3:33 in the morning?"

So I went out and sat down in the middle of the street and faced west and north and east and south simultaneously and waited for 3:33 to come. A whirling wind like a dust devil rotating counter clockwise came down from above and lifted me up into the sky four or five stories and deposited me in a place that I had never been before. The source approached and said for me to walk with him. He told me that he was very pleased with the progress I had made and said that he was giving me a gift, the 'Gift of luxury.'

So, I asked, "Do you mean like lots of money?" He said that money has nothing to do with luxury. "I'm giving you the gift of luxury, the luxury of sleeping undisturbed, the luxury of peace of mind, the luxury of being alive, the luxury of anything you wish to have the luxury of." I asked if I could bestow the gift of luxury on any one else and he said that I could but it would only be for that single thing for that particular event but for myself it applied to anything.

I asked the Source if I still had the gift of healing and the gift of seeing. He said that I had the gift of healing, the gift of seeing, the gift of knowing and the gift of luxury. I thanked him and indulged myself in the gift of sleeping undisturbed. And I made a point of giving myself the gift of living today and enjoying the time I was given being with my family.

Egel

Pronounced (Edge – El)

We had spent the entire day cleaning out the algae infested swimming pool at my son's prior house located in Orange County. The pool had been let go for over a year because the house was un-occupied and the salt cell had stopped working on its chlorine generating system. The filter was clogged with algae and was turned off.

My son finally resorted to pumping all of the algae infested water out ofthe pool with a rented pool pump to start over with fresh clean water after he got the salt cell working and the filter cleaned out. The pool contained almost forty thousand gallons of water so it had taken many hours over several days to get all of the green water out. We finally finished yesterday a little after five o'clock in the afternoon. We packed everything up in the car and left. As we were preparing to leave my son asked me to check later to make sure nothing followed us home from the old house to his new home.

I was tired when I went to bed from working all day cleaning the pool and getting the calcium deposits off of the tile and replacing the missing tiles in the Jacuzzi and forgot to check for any unwanted characters that may have accompanied us home when we left the old house.

I woke up in the middle of the night needing to make a bathroom run. I'm not sure exactly what time it was. I didn't have a clock on the nightstand but I think it was around two o'clock in the morning. The first thing I noticed was a pair of wide set eyes staring at me from out of the darkness. Then, the proverbial, hair on the back of my neck stood up. I knew something was there with me in the pool house where we were sleeping. So, I mobilized the wizard's powers of observation and I saw this large creature next to the bed that could only be described as a cross between a human and a frog. It must have been staying in the green algae infested pool at my son's old house. Now it was here at his new house and I would have to get rid of it. I asked what its name was and it said 'Egel'. I think it was a large male probably weighing several hundred pounds but I knew I would have to get rid of it some how.

At some point I may have to revisit this character to learn from him what his capabilities and limitations are but at the moment I just need to get him out of here before I go back home, so I summoned the wizard's giant and wizard's elf and asked them to find a really nice algae infested place for Egel to stay and personally take him there.

Foot Loose

The other night I visited the Facilitator who was sitting on the park bench next to Lucky, the six year-old boy and Sabatini, the traveler's Buddha facing out on the event horizon. I sat down on the bench next to the Facilitator on his right side between Lucky and him. Sabatini sat on the end of the park bench next to Lucky. The Lion was lying on the sand beside the park bench next to the Facilitator. No one said anything.

Far out on the event horizon there was a twirling disturbance, barely noticeable at first but then rising up

146

out of the water like a whirlwind or short dust devil. We all stood up together simultaneously and moved out over the surface of the water towards the disturbance that was somewhere in the future. When we arrived at the disturbance we joined hands. I held on to the lion with one hand and Lucky with the other hand and the Facilitator held on to the other side of the lion with one hand and Sabatini with the other hand. Sabatini held on to Lucky with his other hand. We formed a circle and began to twirl around in the disturbance.

The disturbance twirled faster and faster. I stepped out of the circle but still remained within the twirling disturbance. I walked back to the park bench and sat down. I could see the disturbance out on the event horizon in the future. Then for the first time I understood my relationship to Lucky, the Facilitator, Sabatini and the giant lion spinning together as one. We were all one. They were each manifestations of myself.

I was foot loose and fancy free.

Victoria

I became involved with Victoria at the request of someone close to her who was very concerned about her desperate situation.

Victoria was an eighteen year old healthy young woman who was swimming in her own pool in her own back yard at around ten o' clock in the morning when she was discovered at the bottom of her pool by her parents who had moments before been talking with her. She was an expert swimmer and swam laps on a daily basis. She was a recent high school graduate who had received a full ride, four-year scholarship to pursue a degree in biochemistry at a prestigious eastern college. She was an outstanding musician and singer and a beautiful young lady. Her whole life lay ahead of her. She was in the hospital on life support after her drowning when I became involved with her.

I went looking for her and found her sitting on the edge of her swimming pool with her feet dangling in the water. She was still wearing her swimsuit. She was very distraught and disoriented. It took some time for her to calm down enough for me to begin to explain the situation to her. I told her that the situation did not look good but there were some things that we could attempt to do if she were willing to go through the trouble and accept the associated risks. When you are on life support your options are few and always fraught with substantial risk. In my personal opinion, there are many situations that are worse than death.

Since neither she nor I had any idea what actually happened that created this situation, I suggested that we go back in time and attempt to use the butterfly effect to alter the outcome. I hoped we could shorten the time between the drowning and the rescue or better yet avoid the whole scenario all together. I told her to get on my back and hold on tight because I didn't want to loose her during the process of traveling back through time and not know where to find her. We arrived back at her home just before the event had taken place and she was swimming laps in the pool.

That was when things got really crazy. This thing that I thought was a demon of some kind, zoomed down in a flash and took Victoria, who was right next to me leaving her body behind sinking in the pool. Victoria was gone for at least fifteen or twenty minutes before she found her way back to the pool where I was waiting. I told her what happened and suggested that we try again only this time I would be better prepared when the thing flashed down out of nowhere.

This time I was waiting holding the wizard's staff with its giant magical blue sapphire jewel on its top at the ready, like a batter waiting for a fast-ball on the outside of the plate. When this thing roared in I whacked it clean out of sight but when I turned around Victoria was gone leaving behind only her sinking body in the pool. It was some time before Victoria made it back to where we had been standing by the pool. I hoped my intervention had altered the outcome and we went to the hospital where I left her on top of her body that was on life support and wished her the best. A few days later she was disconnected from life support. Our efforts had not been successful. The next time I saw Victoria she was exhausted from her futile efforts to re-connect with her own body which had been on life support.

I took her to 'The Place' where I hoped she could restore her energy levels and introduced her to the 'Source' who explained to her the futility of our efforts because of the irreversible brain damage that had occurred. I left them alone having their private and personal conversation. I assumed that she may have been shocked by a short circuit in a light or from touching a radio while still in the water but the Source insisted that it was her fate. When I asked about the demon that had zoomed in and taken her away, he said that it was one of the three Fates that had come for her.

I had heard of the myth of the Three Fates but I didn't believe that they actually existed. The Source even told me where I could find them. They were on an island known as the Island of the Three Fates. With this information I was able to locate the three sisters. The island was tiny and the three sisters were very large and very ugly. One had only a single eye in the middle of her forehead, another had three eyes and the third had five eyes. The one that had come for her was the one with five eyes. The Source told me that it was not possible for me to prevent that fate from taking another person when it was their time but what I had done when I whacked that Fate away was to make it impossible for my Fate to come for me when it was my time to be taken. With that I took Victoria home with me where she has remained. She declined to go to her own funeral. She said that was the past and she needed to move on. Victoria had cut a deal with the Source to reincarnate back into her own family as soon as a suitable baby would be born.

Three Sisters

I visited the three sisters on their tiny little island several times, once as pure awareness, once as a magical crow, once as a giant eagle and once as a giant wizard with a huge magical staff, which I used to whack each of them off their island and into some unknown distant place; thereby preventing all three of the sisters of Fate from having any control over my future or my fate. That would leave my ultimate fate remaining in my own hands and my hands alone.

I looked on the Internet to see if there was any information there about the three Fate Sisters. This is what I found.

The Greeks believed that there were three Fates. "Clotho spun the thread of human fate, Lachesis dispensed it and Atropos cut the thread, thus determining the individual's moment of death."

The Roman goddesses were named, Nona, Decuma and Morta. They were referred to as the Moirai. They were three sister deities, incarnations of destiny and life. They were thought to be the daughters of Zeus and the Titan goddess Themis. It was believed that the Moirai would visit the house three days after a child was born and determine that child' s fate and life.

Moiragetes translates as 'he who commands the Fates'. Supposedly only Zeus was capable of controlling the actions of these three sisters of Fate. But apparently I am now immune to their actions because I whacked each of them off of their island and they no longer have any power over me.

When I first encountered them, before I knew their names, I called them Bertha, Jayden and Thom.

Ardyth Simpson

This morning early, a little after midnight I asked Victoria if she wanted to go with me to 'The Place'. I was going to meditate there. She wanted to come with me so we had just situated ourselves there when the Source asked us to walk with him. He took us to a place that was green and lush with vegetation. We stopped at a split rail fence with what appeared to be a small farmhouse in the distance on the other side. He asked Victoria what she saw. She said that she didn't see anything. The Source asked me what I saw. On the other side of the fence there was a large field with tall grass and spring flowers of all kinds. Beyond the field there was a small, very small, wooden farmhouse. The Source told me to take Victoria over to the small house. Inside everything looked rather plain and antiquated. We looked all around the place and then left. When I turned around Victoria was gone.

I asked the Source where she was. He told me that she was staying there. That was where she was re-incarnated on the 28th of October 1937 in Winona, Wisconsin. Her name was Ardyth Simpson. She was born at home in that farmhouse. She became a piano teacher and is still living somewhere. I asked the

Source about Victoria wanting to be born back into her own family. He said that she was offered the chance to be her sister's child but she refused that opportunity and was re-assigned to this parallel life yet unfinished. I asked the Source why Victoria was unable to see what I saw. He said that she had already had her memory of her last existence wiped clean in preparation for her next life, besides she was not accustomed to time travel like I was and she was unable to process things from another time.

The Loft

At 4:43 a.m. this morning I went out to the street in front of our house and sat down in the middle of the pavement facing west, and north and east and south and up and down simultaneously. At 4:44 a.m. the scaffolding of the matrix appeared. Out of the matrix a stairs formed. I climbed the stairs that ended in a circular room with doors all around it. Only one door had writing on it. That was the door I opened. It said 'Wizards'. On the other side there was nothing, absolutely nothing. I closed the door behind me and an old fashion, antique, oak, roll-top desk appeared. It was open and on the desk an inkwell complete with a quill sticking out of it appeared. I sat down at the desk and picked up the quill. A large piece of parchment appeared. I put the quill down on the paper and it began to write. "From this day forward you are now and forever officially to be known as the 'Sapphire Blue Wizard.' This place is your official 'Wizard's Loft' from which your wizardry will emanate."

I wondered where that all came from. Perhaps it was an inspiration. Perhaps it was just wishful thinking. Only time will tell.

Justification

I believe everything does happen for some reason. Eventually we usually get some idea of what the real reason is in time. My initial assumptions about things rarely turn out to be accurate.

The three books in this trilogy are connected by a single theme. This single purpose was news to me until now. I'm sure it will be quite disturbing for you as well. Remember this saying, "Don't kill the messenger!"

All of these challenges and adventures that I have shared with you have given me the skill sets necessary to prepare me to plead the case for humanity. Our planet has been quarantined and our species has been slated for extinction. The Galactic Council has already decided our fate. My task is to get them to reconsider that decision. I have visited the future and it looks really bad for us. Thirty-nine years from now in 2056 there will only be a little more than fifty-six thousand humans still alive on earth. I hope this isn't the best deal I could work out with the Galactic Council on our behalf.

Tiny

Tiny, the tiny Titan was not his real name. He had been the biggest, the baddest and the meanest of the Titans. Everyone feared him. He always won at whatever he did. He thought that he was a great leader but none of those qualities endear anyone.

It is true that Titans are extremely large and physically very powerful but I needed a leader who could garner trust and maintain order and fidelity to the task at hand. That would require wisdom, faith and perseverance. That would require complete and total trust in their leader. I hoped that I could bring out these qualities in this young Titan. He was a perfect physical specimen but he needed lots of work.

Wizard Island was home to Titans. But Wizard Island only existed when there was a wizard there in residence. Otherwise it ceased to exist. I knew that the island would not be complete until the Titans returned.

I first brought Aurora and then Alex to the island. Next I brought two of their friends and then the two mothers of the two young females over. That made for a total of six Titans. They have been working diligently to clean the place up and get it ready for more Titans to come over to Wizard Island from deep in the past where they now reside.

Next I brought over the least of the Titans. He was the smallest and the weakest and the most disrespected among them. I showed him everything to prepare him for his return to the Titans as their informant.

Before I took the weakest Titan back I asked each of the seven Titans who they would like for me to bring back next. Each and every one of the seven said whatever you do don't bring back the one I call Tiny because they all feared him.

So that was the one I brought back with me when I took the weakest Titan back and left him there to tell the rest of the Titans about Wizard Island and the future they could have there in the home of their ancestors.

I brought this huge powerful Titan specimen back and shrank him to the size of a midget and left him to accommodate and adapt to being the smallest weakest most dependent among them. After six weeks of this experience he was open to having a serious discussion about assuming the leadership of the Titans with a personal appreciation for what it means to serve others for only the leader who thinks of all and cares for the smallest and weakest among them has any chance of becoming a great leader who is worthy of followers.

With that I returned him to his Titan Clan in this his diminutive state with the admonition that he must convince as many Titans as possible to come to Wizard Island for that was their only chance to return to the land of their ancestors. I told him that I would bring the other Titans one at a time as they chose to come to Wizard's Island.

Mantor & Lyle

I returned Tiny, not his real name, to where all the other Titans were a week or so ago. His task was to convince as many Titans as possible to leave where they were in the distant past and to take a chance on me bringing them into the future and leaving them on Wizard Island the original homeland of the Titans.

I went back last night to see if anyone had been convinced to take him up on this proposition. Mantor and Lyle chose to come with me in hopes for a better life far into the future. Mantor turned out to be the oldest living Titan. He wanted to have the opportunity to spend the final days of his life and to die in his ancestral homeland. That seemed quite logical to me so I brought him back to Wizard Island and introduced him to everyone and explained to them his hopes and aspirations.

Lyle on the other hand was much younger and his reason or reasons to leave where he was, so to speak, were very different. He wasn't as much interested in coming to Wizard Island as he was in leaving where he was far back in the distant past. He was what we might call a conscientious objector, to all sorts of things. Lyle believed that the Titans were engaged in conflicts at the behest of others and that they were needlessly dying for ridiculous reasons. He felt that no one was listening to his concerns and he didn't like the place where the Titans were stuck in both time and place. Ergo he was willing to take a chance with a total stranger who promised to transport him to another time and another place far from where he formerly was living.

Two days later when I returned, there were seven older female Titans waiting to be transported far into the future to live out their remaining years on Wizard Island, home of the mythical Titans.

Last night I brought a group of thirty Titans across one at a time. That makes a total of forty-three Titans living now where they belong, on Wizard Island.

Deming

This morning, at 2:00 o'clock I went out to the street in front of our house to see if anything was going on. There was a stagecoach stopped right in front of our driveway. I climbed on board and the coach began moving. It was bouncing along down a rutted dusty road not much more than a trail barely wide enough for a horse drawn wagon.

Sitting directly across facing me was a cowboy with a long mustache who could have used a bath and a shave. He said. "Where ya headed, pardner?" No body in their right mind goes to Deming so I said, "El Paso," "And you?" He replied, "Durango." We bounced along in silence. I put my head back and pulled my Stetson hat down over my eyes like I was sleeping. Sitting next to me on my left side was a nicely dressed young lady maybe in her thirties. Before long I felt those delicate hands checking my pockets for any loose cash or a watch and my belt for a hidden purse.

I reached down slowly with my right hand and pulled my Colt 380 automatic that I always carry, out of my boot and the delicate little hands vanished. The cowboy retorted, "What is that? I've never seen nuttin like that in my life!"

I dropped the clip into my lap with a flick of my thumb, pulled the slide, opened the breach and handed it to the cowboy butt first without lifting my hat off from over my eyes. He was totally in shock for nothing like that would be invented in his lifetime.

The stagecoach came rumbling to a halt. The driver yelled out "Deming". I got up and said, "This is my stop."

The shocked cowboy blurted out, "Where you from, pardner?"

I smiled and said, as I relieved him of my semi-automatic 380 Colt pistol, "The future... The future." And, I got down from the stagecoach we were riding in.

There was not much more than a saloon and a livery stable in Deming. I made my way into the saloon and sat dawn at the bar put my automatic pistol on the counter in front of me and ordered a drink with my two fingers. The patrons stared at me in my clean suit and new red boots. They all thought I was a gambler for sure. The bartender said twenty-five cents. I chugged the two fingers of whisky and smacked down a shiny two thousand and seventeen quarter and got up to leave. The bartender said, "Where you from man?"

I replied, "The future man... The future" and I disappeared.

Deming is a town in New Mexico located in Luna County thirty-three miles north of Mexico and sixty miles west of Las Cruces. In 1850 it was a Butterfield Stage stop.

Nine Faces

I was busy last night doing onsite research for the next book, 'Star Quest: Navigator'. I was tired and felt I should go to 'The Place' and recharge. I situated myself there in the silence and emptiness when all of a sudden, one face after another popped up in front of me. There were a total of nine different faces. Some were African. Some were from Mexico or South America. Some were from the sub-continent. One was Aborigine. One was a boy about nine years of age. All were of brown skin color. None were white and none were black, only different shades of brown. They were all males. One had ornamental scars all around his face. At that point, the Source appeared.

I asked him who all the faces were. He asked me who I thought they were. I told him that I thought they were all prophets or seers. A door appeared out of nothingness. The Source said the answer lay behind that door. I got up from where I was sitting, walked over to the door and opened it.

On the other side of the door was a cave that sloped downward. I entered the cave and the door vanished leaving me standing in the middle of the sloping cave. I walked down the cave until it ended in a pool of water. The cave was obviously flooded. I stared into the surface of the water and I could see movement beneath its surface. I put my face into the water and I was completely under the water staring up at its surface.

I was in a medical office of some kind but it wasn't my office. A young blond teen-age girl came up to me and said,"Now you have found the gateway to Prophecy."

Everything vanished in an instant and I was lying on my back in bed staring up at the dark ceiling above.

Prophecy

Last night I worked on several projects before going to 'The Place' to recharge. While I was there I decided to check out the door that led to the tunnel. At first the tunnel appeared to be the same but when I arrived at the area that was flooded, the water was all gone. Perhaps something I did drained it away. Instead of water there was an enlarged opening in the tunnel that was about fifteen feet in diameter. That's how the tunnel ended. I sat down in the middle of the enlarged area. The nine faces from the night before complete with their bodies appeared. The young nine-year old boy stood right in front of me.

I asked him if he were a seer or a prophet. He asked me, "What's the difference."

I said to him that I wasn't sure if there was a difference.

He said, "A seer sees ... a prophet tells others what he has seen." Then, he disappeared. Each of the other eight seers and prophets disappeared after they shared their own perspectives regarding prophecy. The one next to the boy on his right side, my left side, was an Aborigine, with tear drop ornamental scars across his forehead and down onto his face. When I turned my attention to him he said, "A seer sees with his eyes. A prophet speaks with his mouth." Then, he too disappeared.

Standing next to the boy on his left side, which was my right, there was a Tibetan monk. He proclaimed, "My eyes know many things. My lips speak only kindness." With these words, he too disappeared. Next to him, to his left, was a Native American medicine man. I immediately recognized him. He said to me, "We are all of many minds but of one spirit." Then he vanished.

Next to the Aborigine on his right side stood a tall witch doctor. He appeared to be from the Caribbean. He had lots of strange tattoos and ornamental scars everywhere. He held a small object tightly in his left hand. It appeared to be a voodoo doll. He said, "A seer breathes air. A prophet breathes only fire." Then, he was gone.

Next to him was an African witch doctor. He said, "See with your eyes. Speak with your lips but touch only with your heart." Then he vanished.

Next to the Native American medicine man was an Indian from South America. He could have been an Inca but I couldn't say for sure. He said to me, "Your feet know the path they should follow. Your tongue knows the story it should tell but your mind moves too much." With that he also vanished. Next to him stood an Arab, one with a thin sharp nose dressed as a Persian. He said only, "The answer lies in your mind."

The last one who was standing behind me, directly opposite the young boy, looked like he was from India. He was barefoot and without a shirt. His long matted hair and beard contrasted with his tattered loincloth. He reached out and touched my forehead saying, "I give you now, the gift of prophecy" then he too vanished.

Exodus

Last night I ventured back to where the Titans were located deep in the past to see if anymore of them wanted to journey with me into the future and live on Wizard Island. Only three more of them had chosen to take such a chance with a stranger. At this rate it would take forever to get them all out of where they were and into an alternative future. Where they were now would soon become their doom.

So this is what I did. I gave the tiny Titan the deep booming voice of the God of thunder to urge them onward. I had Gem the Wizard's Elf hold open one end of a time-tunnel that was on Wizard Island and I had the Wizard's Giant hold open the other end of the time-tunnel where all the Titans were now living. The other thing I did to help convince all of the Titans to get moving was to increase the size of the now tiny Titan to twice his original size making him a giant Titan with the voice of thunder. That combination did the trick. All of the other Titans began funneling into the time-tunnel and exiting on their true home of destiny on Wizard Island. The Titan who had been the smallest and weakest of them led them to safety. The tiny Titan, Alexander, who was originally the largest and strongest of the Titans but was shrunk by me into a tiny Titan and then turned into a giant Titan with a thunderous voice took up the rear and followed the last of the Titans as they left their past behind and embraced their common future together on Wizard Island.

I closed the portal as the Giant and I passed trough its opening thus terminating the time-tunnel preventing anything else from going to Wizard Island. Gem the elf held the other end of the tunnel open until the Giant and I passed through.

Flora & Sam

Last week my son called and said that he and my granddaughter had gone swimming at their old house and brought something home with them to their new house. He didn't know what it was or where it was located but he believed that whatever they brought home with them was causing problems. I told him I would come over later that evening and see what we could do to get rid of his the new visitors.

The group that I assembled for this project included the following: The lion, the Facilitator, Lucky the young boy, Sabatini the traveler's Buddha, the wizard's elf, the wizards giant and myself. All of us transported over together from my back yard to the street in front of his house. Lucky and I took the inside of the property. Sabatini took up the lookout position high above the property and the remaining four members of the team each took up their positions on the four corners of the property.

The first thing I noticed was that the swimming pool was yellow instead of being blue. That was a give away. Something had to be in their swimming pool. The thing swimming around there appeared to be a tall transparent blond woman wearing a long flowing yellow gown that was iridescent and shimmering. It flowed like the long fins of a fancy gold fish or Koi. I got her out of the pool and began to question her. She told me her name was Flora and she was known as the 'Flapping Fish' because of the way she moved her arms up and down like a bird flying when she was in the water. Supposedly she was the embodiment of stuttering. That was not going to work out around my five-year old granddaughter. I would have to get rid of her. The last thing I need is a granddaughter that has a stuttering problem.

Lucky and I went through the whole property and the entire house and found a small pudgy little guy less than two feet tall in the family room. He said that his name was Sam. He told me that he was the embodiment of the drifter. There was no place for him either at my son's house. I got rid of both of them in a hurry.

The Hammer

My son who lives in Orange County called last night while we were watching a movie on the DVD player. He and his daughter had been swimming at his old house that was being renovated that afternoon. He thought that they might have picked something up while they were there and asked me to come over and check it out. I told him I would be over later to see what I could find.

It was almost midnight when I organized the expedition party. The members were the same as the last time I went over when we encountered Flora and Sam. Our group consisted of the lion, the Facilitator, the six-year old boy Lucky, Sabatini, the Traveler's Buddha; Gem the wizard's elf; Ned the wizard's giant and myself. We left from my back yard and assembled in the street in front of my son's house.

The formation was similar to our last encounter here at my son's house. The lion, the Facilitator, the elf and the giant covered the four corners of the property. Sabatini was positioned high above in the center of the property. Lucky and I started going around and around the property from the perimeter inward, in opposite directions. Lucky circled to the right and I circled to the left. We went through everything even the crawl spaces under the house and in the attic. We found nothing. I had everyone withdraw to a safe distance and I detonated two psychic bombs that would get rid of anything that we might have missed in our search. The first bomb was placed in the swimming pool. Nothing flew out of there when that bomb went off. The second bomb was detonated in the center of the interior of the house. A single object went flying out of the house and flew far up into the air.

Usually I leave things at that but I was curious as to what this thing was. It appeared to be a small disc about seven or eight inches in diameter. So, I pursued it, caught up with it and stuffed it into the leather bag that I always carry with me. I didn't know what it was or what I should do with it. I thought about several possibilities but finally decided it would probably be safe to take it to the moon and leave it there on the moon's surface.

Once there, I opened the bag and took the object out an examined it. To me it looked like two, glazed earthenware saucers glued together face to face to form a disc. The surface was fairly smooth and regular. The color was not quite as yellow as Dijon mustard. It was a little more tannish in color. I would describe it as two antique saucers glued together. I began asking it

167

questions. What are you? Where did you come from? What were you doing at my son's house? What are you capable of doing? The questioning went on and on ad nauseam. This is what I was told: It was the embodiment of the breaker of dinner plates. It was created in the distant past specifically to break plates. This sounded really weird to me and so the story continues.

Apparently my son's house was built on or near a fault line, which is a crack in the earth where one side of the fault moves in a different direction from the other side of the fault. There also was a rift in time that ran right through his property and his house. I have heard of a wrinkle in time or a distortion in time but I have never heard of a rift. This discontinuity apparently allows things from one location in time to find their way into another place in time.

I thought the best thing that I could do with this disc was to return it to its creator. We used this rift in time to get there. I was shocked to see who or what had created this strange disc and his motivation for creating it was even more bizarre. This character was absolutely huge. It was at least twenty feet tall and almost twelve feet wide. It looked like a supersized hulk with bronzed skin and long dark hair. It had no shirt on and wore no shoes. It was standing in front of what we would think of as a gigantic anvil of sorts. In his right hand he wielded a supper size hammer with a flat square head. When he smashed it down on whatever he was working on sparks showered out in every direction accompanied by an earth-shaking BOOM.

I presented the disc to this giant and asked why he had created it in the first place. He was obviously some sort of God or demi God. He said that long ago he visited a village on earth. Instead of offering him a plate of food, as was the universal custom when a stranger visited your community or your home in those times, they offered him nothing. As a God he was insulted and created this disc, which would break the favorite dinner plates of humans. I asked him if he were the God of thunder. He said that he was. I know that the Thunder God goes by many names. When I asked him what name he wanted me to address him by he said, "Call me THE HAMMER." I left the small round disc with him and returned to my own time. It started to rain at my house. There was a brilliant lightning flash that was quickly followed by a tremendous boom and all the doors and windows rattled. Then there was another and another and another. These were nothing like anything I have ever experienced before. The thunder God made a believer out of me in short order.

I got the idea that perhaps if Kim Jong Un experienced what I just experienced he might think twice about lobbing a bunch of missiles at Guam. So I returned to where the Thunder God was busily working and asked if he would be so kind as to give Kim Jong Un a demonstration like he had just given me. He said that he would. After I got back home I got an encore of flashes and booms from THE HAMMER.

The next day Kim Jong Un disappeared. He was not to be seen anywhere in public.

The next day after that Kim Jung Un cancelled his launch of four missiles aimed at Guam.

It was probably just a coincidence…then again perhaps not.

Chamber of Echoes

Last night I went to Gliese 180 b twice to gather more information about that planet. Doing that tends to deplete my energy reserves so I went to 'The Place' to recharge my energy supply. While I was there I was talking with the Source.

Just outside of 'The Place' two doors appeared, one on the left and one on the right. The door on the left leads to the tunnel of prophecy. The door on the right leads to the chamber where the connections between all things coalesce. The Source asked which of the two doors I chose to enter.

My response was that there was a third door, which should also be there but was missing. The Source wanted to know what door that might be. I told him the door leading to the 'Oracle'. That door magically appeared and I left 'The Place' and entered therein. When I did so a round room lined with doors appeared. It was the Chamber of Echoes. I called out to the Oracle and I could hear his voice echoing around the room with many, many doors. He was in distress. I had to go to him but I had no idea which door would lead to where he was more than two thousand years in the past. With my newly obtained wizardly powers I knew that it was the second door from the left and entered through that door.

I found myself in the Oracle's cave. He was in a desperate condition, near death. I rushed to his side and administered a magical potion that I always carry with me, which can counteract any poison. He began immediately to recover. The Oracle told me that Isaiah had brought him a plate of food that was laced with poison. His mistress was probably behind the whole thing. I recovered the poison from the Oracle and suggested that I poison Isaiah with it. Then I suggested that we poison his mistress with it. Then I placed the small vial of poison in my pocket and said that each and everyone gets what they have coming, sooner or later and it wasn't my place to mete out another's punishment. I saved the Oracle's life and that was what really mattered in the end. I returned to The Place. The Source said, "I am pleased that you focused only on the positive. Well done."

Flaming Blue Suit

Later in the morning I woke up in the middle of a crazy lucid dream. I was wearing a suit and I was on fire and completely covered in blue flames. I thought, this cannot be a good thing. Later when I was talking with the Source I asked him what the point of the blue flames was. He said for me to go with him.

We walked through this small portico into a small spherical space. He said, "You are entering the Holiest of Holy places. This is the Orb of Sanctity, the Sphere of Security. Inside this space evil can never find you."

I asked again what the point was of me being burned alive by the blue flames. He said that the blue flames burned away all my iniquities and purified me so that I would be cleansed and could enter unhindered into this sacred space.

I don't know. It might take a lot of burning to do that.

Death Ray

Last night I went to 'The Place,' which is something I do almost every night. When I was ready to leave those same three doors appeared. I chose to enter the door on the left which has the word PROPHECY written on it in large black letters. I went down the sloping tunnel to the round room at its end and sat down in the middle of the room to meditate.

The image of a flying saucer appeared above me hovering in the distance. It didn't appear like flying saucers as they are depicted in science fiction movies.

It was like the space ship I encountered a few years ago that was about one hundred and fifty yards in diameter with fat rounded edges and no windows. It was dark grey in color and looked like it was made of a series of skinny bicycle inner tubes of decreasing diameters stacked on top and bottom to form a symmetrical saucer shape. The date that it is suppose to first appear is on November 3, 2047.

The next date that was disclosed was October 2048. At that time there were many of theses flying saucers spread out in a dispersed formation. The saucer that was closest to me sent out a reddish yellow beam of energy that spread out as it left the ship and increased in diameter before it hit its target. I don't think it was a laser because it was continuous in duration not intermittent and was reddish as it left the spacecraft but was a bright yellow when it reached its target.

Supposedly by the year 2056 there will only be 56 thousand plus a few hundred human beings alive on planet earth. I assumed that we would kill each other off with our own nuclear weapons or maybe be done in by some virulent strain of deadly virus. But this death ray thing is quite objectionable to me so I ventured to where the Galactic Council was in session and voiced my concern. The council disregarded my interruption so I proceeded from left to right and demonstrated my displeasure by blowing the head off of the first council member, blowing the right hand off of the second member, blowing the left hand off of the third member, blowing both hands off of the fourth member, blowing the right leg off of the fifth member, blowing the left leg off of the sixth member, blowing both legs off of the seventh member, blowing the right arm off of the eighth member, blowing the left arm off of the ninth member, blowing both legs and both arms off of the tenth member, and blowing the body off of the eleventh member leaving only his head lying on the table.

Subsequently I restored all of the members of the council to their former state of being and restated my objection to their plans to terminate the human race with a Death Ray. I conceded that humans have no redeeming qualities and probably do deserve to be exterminated but this Death Ray thing was a totally unacceptable approach to me.

I can assure you they were dumbfounded by what they all experienced and had no idea how I could have pulled that process off. But that is because they know nothing of wizardry, magic and the power of illusion.

Dealer's Deck

As I left 'The Place' last night, the Source asked me to walk with him. We walked a short ways until we came upon a very small table for two with a deck of cards placed face down on one side. The Source asked me to sit down and two chairs appeared out of thin air.

We sat down at the dealer's table. The Source spread the cards smoothly in an ark across the table with one movement of his hand. He then asked me to pick a card. I picked one from the middle and turned it over. It was a Queen of Spades. He asked me to pick another card. I chose another card and turned it over. It was the Jack of Diamonds. Again he wanted me to pick another card. I picked another card and turned it over. It was the Ace of Hearts. One final time the Source asked me to pick another card. I did so and it turned out to be the three of Clubs.

The Source leaned back in his chair and asked me what I thought of the cards I had chosen. I looked at them and looked back at him and said that I didn't think anything of the cards. The Source told me that those were my cards. That was my hand and they represented my life. He then turned all of the other cards over facing up. They were all blank. There was nothing on any of them. He waited for me to give him an answer. I said that I had no idea what the cards meant. I knew nothing about the cards.

The Source then elaborated. The Queen of Spades represents the women in your life. They have always come first before anything else. The Jack of Diamonds represents you, a jack-of-all-trades, a diamond in the rough. The Ace of Hearts represents the love you have for all creatures, great and small. The three of Clubs are the three doors that wait for you just outside 'The Place'. The door to the left is the Door of Prophecy. The door in the center is the Door to the Oracle and the door to your right is the Door to the connection between all things, past, present & future. These cards represent your life. They are your cards, your hand and you have chosen to play them.

The Source vanished. I picked up the deck of blank cards and turned them over. On each card was the face of a woman, all of the women in my life who have had a hand in creating who I am and what I am capable of doing. On the very first card was a picture of my mother.

Four Black Crows

A couple of days ago my son who lives in Orange County called and told me that my granddaughter had a nightmare early that morning where crows were attacking her. I told him I would be over later and see what the problem was. When I got there it was a little after midnight. I went alone to evaluate the situation.

In my granddaughter's bedroom I discovered four giant black crows. I knew right away that they were sorcerers and not giant black crows. They all rushed towards me at once. I proceeded to knock each one of them 'out of the park' with my wizard's staff. I didn't give it much thought but I did decide to ask a sorcerer friend of mine to look into it and let me know what she found out about the four crows being there.

Last night I visited the sorceress in the year 1756 and asked her what she found out about the four crows. She said they were not crows at all but in fact sorcerers, which was something I suspected already. She said that the four sorcerers had gone to my granddaughter's bedroom and set up a trap for me because they knew I would be coming over there. They believed that the four of them could overpower me and steal my magic from me because they thought I was still a wizardling with no real wizardly powers. They were wrong. I am a wizard, the 'Sapphire Blue Wizard' and I easily overpowered all of them and in the process absorbed all of their powers leaving them as powerless old men to live out the remainder of their lives as four hapless derelicts.

I thanked the sorceress for her information as we danced the night away to the music we could hear playing in our minds.

Six-guns

Early this morning before 1:00 o'clock I went outside to the driveway and stood under the street lamp to see if the night plane would be passing by. Nothing was happening so I sat down on the edge of the street and waited. I was anticipating the sound of some kind of airplane approaching in the distance. Instead I heard the unmistakable clop, clop clopping of a horse's hoofs on the hard asphalt surface of the road.

The horse stopped near by me. When I looked up the rider had dismounted and whipped out both of his pistols as he appeared from behind his horse. He stood directly in front of me with both of his guns pointed straight at my forehead. I recognized this cowboy from an encounter two years ago on this same street right in front of my house. He was a past incarnation of myself. He was the "Lone Rider" from the first book of the trilogy, "Coincidental Journey".

The Lone Rider spun the pistols backwards on his trigger fingers then slapped them down on the ground in front of me with their barrels pointed directly at me. Without speaking a single word he remounted his steed and whorled his horse around and they slowly plodded back down the road the way they had come. I watched them as they moved towards the 'T' intersection at the end of our street. As they entered the intersection they vanished into a shimmering mirage. I picked up the two pistols and spun them deftly backwards around my trigger fingers. They felt like extensions of my own hands, as though I had done it before a thousand times. They were a matched pair of pearl-handled Colt long-barrel 44's. I took them into the house with me and placed them gingerly on the floor next to my nightstand. I asked the Source what the whole encounter was really all about. He told me that I should take them with me where ever I traveled because I would need them to protect myself. He also reminded me of the necessity of establishing contact with all of my past incarnations. This can most readily be accomplished by crossing over "The Wizard's Bridge" and onto the other side of the "Abyss".

Ezekiel

I took the advice of the Source and crossed over the Wizard's Bridge and stepped right into a gathering of my many past lives just to the right side of the end of the bridge. All of the different characters that comprised my total life's experiences were milling around there. Before I was able to engage any of them in conversation, there was a disturbance directly in front of me in the distance that distracted everyone's attention. Out of the darkness emerged a tall bearded man wearing a floor length hooded robe. He held a small bundle of clothing under his arm. It was neatly tied up with a gold colored sash. Everyone stared at him as he moved closer and closer.

He stopped directly in front of me and addressed me as 'Michael the Wizard'. He told me that his name was Ezekiel and that I was a re-incarnation of himself. He said that he was a wizard from the distant past who was one of the four wizards residing on Wizard Island. He was forced to leave the island when conflict between the four wizards erupted. He as well as the other three wizards misused their powers and were misguided in their actions, which resulted in all four of the wizards, as well as all the Titans being forced into exile. He said that I was not the 'Sapphire Blue Wizard.' I could not assume the identity of another wizard. I was Michael the Wizard of the South. He presented to me an off-white ivory-colored robe of soft wool with a gold sash. The matching wizard's hat was adorned with stars and moons and planets of gold, as were the matching shoes with pointed toes. I asked about the wizard's staff. He said that each wizard must acquire their own personal staff through their own effort. I surrendered the sapphire blue wizard's staff to

Ezekiel. He informed me that Wizard Island needed all four wizards in order for the full power of the island to be realized. It was up to me to gather three more wizards and bring them to the island. All of that power would be needed to accomplish the task set before me, to keep the Galactic Council from exterminating all human life here on Earth.

Ocotillo

Last night after restoring my energy in 'The Place' I asked the Source if he could provide me with any insight regarding my challenge of finding three more wizards to join together with me on Wizard Island. He said, "The answer lies within 'The Golden Fleece.' You need to leave the outfit for the Wizard of the South on Wizard Island. You cannot go anywhere dressed as a wizard without a wizard's staff."

I had given the Golden Fleece to Father Time a year or so ago. I was also told by Ezekiel the wizard and Jacomo the creator of the balsamo wizard's staff that the staff chooses the wizard as does the specific stone that is placed atop of that staff. So, I need to find a staff and a stone that chooses me and not the other way around, before I can recruit three other wizards for Wizard Island. This whole process was challenging for me even to begin the task.

At 2:00 o'clock in the morning I went out to catch a ride on the Night Bus. The bus was waiting for me with its doors open. I climbed on board and told Brad, the raccoon bus driver, I needed to go to the jungle. He wanted to know what jungle. I told him the one I went to where I found Sabatini and the Sapphire Blue Wizard. He told me to go to the very back of the bus and sit in the middle of the seat and not to forget to put on the seat belt. I didn't even know that this old bus had seat belts and I had never used one before.

He started off slowly, as we hit speed bump after speed bump in the seemingly endless process of bouncing along. When we finally stopped I fell out of the back of the bus and into a dense jungle. I climbed the nearest tall tree to get a lay of the land. As far as the eye could see in every direction there was endless jungle with the exception of a small pointed peak not terribly far off in one direction. That is where I headed. It took quite a while to get there traveling through the dense underbrush but I finally made it.

The jungle ended at the base of the small mountain. It was very steep and rocky but the vegetation was sparse. Near the top of the peak I came across what looked like a narrow dirt road in a very bad state of repair. There was an old car sitting on the road occupied by three young women and a young boy. I asked if they could give me a lift but they were reluctant to do so. On the other side of the mountain I could see a large town. I told them I would help them with whatever they were trying to do there on the mountain if they would give me a ride down the mountain and into the town. The mountain was very different than the jungle around it. It was like a dry desert with not much vegetation on it and the plants were from the Sonoran desert. They told me they were clearing away vegetation in preparation for building a house overlooking the city below. They asked me to move this giant ocotillo plant that was more than twenty feet tall. I agreed and as I began to dig away at the roots of the ocotillo the large central stem separated itself from the rest of the plant. Its roots were wrapped around a large cluster of pure quartz crystals laced together with veins of pure gold.

This was to be fashioned into my own personal wizard's staff. I cut off a section containing the eight roots that wrapped around the quartz crystal and the strong straight stem about eight feet in length. When I held it in my hands above my head and shook off the dirt still clinging to the roots I was transported instantly to my house. I took my future wizard's staff into 'The Place' and left it there. When I returned it was a beautifully transformed ocotillo wizard's staff, my wizard's staff.

Fleecing Time

The next night I went to visit Father Time to ask about the Golden Fleece. I told him what the Source had said that the answers lay within the Golden Fleece. He immediately retrieved it from deep within his cave and gave it to me. He told me to wear it over my shoulders. He said it would help me to achieve my objectives. From there I went to see Merlin the magician who was living in Ireland in the Glen, which he had recently completed restoring to its original state. I told him that I needed to find three wizards to join me on Wizard Island. He said there were no living wizards and that I would need to travel deep into the past to find any. Merlin provided detailed directions on how I could locate them. Me wearing the Golden Fleece over my shoulders gave the three wizards the confidence to travel with me back to Wizard Island.

From there I revisited Father Time to return his precious Golden Fleece. Father Time thanked me for returning the fleece promptly but insisted that I keep it and wear it under my wizard's robe because it would provide me with the power needed to manage the three wizards and the army of Titans back on Wizard Island.

Harvest Moon

Yesterday was the night of the full moon, the Festival of the Harvest Moon. We ate Moon Cakes and watched the full moon, the harvest moon, in all its radiant beauty.

It was also the night of the full moon when the magic crows use to come bearing gifts for me. They were giant crows that were actually shape shifting sorcerers but they stopped coming to my house on their monthly visits bearing gifts when I was no longer an ordinary sorcerer but a wizardling, a novice wizard learning the ways of a wizard, which are markedly different than the ways of a sorcerer. I was ex-communicated. I was blackballed. I was thrown out of the International Murder of Magical Crows.

I went to visit a magical crow that I know in the 18th century. I asked her if she planned on going to the gathering of magical crows tonight on the night of the full moon. She said that she had planned on going soon. I told her that once she got there I would be able to find her and come to where she was. She should pretend that she and I don't know each other.

When I appeared I was wearing my off-white wizard's attire emblazoned with gold suns and moons and planets carrying my ocotillo wizard's staff topped with its quartz crystals interlaced with veins of pure gold radiating energy. One by one the giant magical crows popped and returned to individual sorcerers.

I reminded them all that I was Michael, former King of the Magical Crows who was now Michael the White Wizard of the South. I had gathered the Titans and re-populated Wizard Island with them, as well as three other wizards and myself. Together we were tasked with convincing the Galactic Council to reverse their decree to terminate all human life on earth.

It would be in everyone's best interest for all of the magic crows to become active participants with me in accomplishing this goal. They became giant black crows again, scattering in every direction. I met up with the sorceress in Spain. She was in her early forties, tall, slender, with jet-black hair and dark-brown eyes. I asked her why she never married and was always alone. She was extremely attractive and could have married well. She bluntly stated that if she had married, her husband would have enslaved her. She would have had child after child, been forced to clean his house, feed his animals and cook for him and his children, do his laundry and do his bidding, suffer in silence and endure all things without pay. She has her point but she is still a beautiful woman.

Ivory Wash

Another month has passed. The full moon in November was supposed to be on the 3rd. The Magical crows have long since stopped coming to my house on the night of the full moon. I don't want to loose all contact with the magical crows. They are after all consummate shape shifting sorcerers. I went outside after midnight on the morning of the 3rd of November but no crows appeared, so I went back in time to visit the sorceress in the year 1756. I asked her where the official gathering of the International Order of Magical Crows was going to be on this full moon. She told me that it was going to be from 9:00 o'clock p.m. this evening until three o'clock in the morning on the 4th of November at the Ivory Wash. I of course had no idea where the Ivory Wash was located or even what the Ivory Wash was. She said she would meet me there.

I reminded her to pretend like she didn't know me because it could cause trouble for her because I have been officially blackballed.

It was after midnight before I arrived at the Ivory Wash. I had no idea what to expect the Ivory Wash would be. When I arrived many thousands of magical crows were milling around near an elevated platform with stairs going up on the left side and another stairs going down off of the platform on the right side. There were no handrails or guardrails on the stairs or on the elevated platform, only a single post like a hangman's gallows with a single disc shaped shower-head from which an ivory colored liquid would squirt down on each individual crow as it came up from the stairs on the left, stopped momentarily under the shower head where it was sprayed with the ivory colored liquid then it would depart from the platform down the stairs on the right side.

After each crow was sprayed with the ivory liquid it would join up with all of the other sprayed crows forming an ever-increasing group. At first I was unable to distinguish the sprayed crows from the unsprayed crows still waiting their turn at the gallows to be sprayed. With my wizards powers of observation I could see that the sprayed crows were all iridescent in the moonlight. There was no way for me to not take my turn at the ivory wash shower. But, I waited to be the very last crow to do so.

I walked nonchalantly up to the showerhead, was sprayed for an extra long time then walked forward and bowed until my black beak touched the floor. I transformed into the white wizard and stopped time. I strode around the gathering of magical crows with my wizard's staff completely encircling them as I scribed two concentric lines one clockwise and one counter clockwise before returning to the platform and restarting time.

The crows on the outside of the gathering of crows began to take flight one after the other in a clockwise direction like dominos strung together in a spiral. The crows on the inside of the gathering began to do likewise but in a counter-clockwise direction. They formed two spirals one inside of the other as they circled upward inside a column of moonlight formed by the November full moon. It was an amazing site to behold.

From there I returned to the sorceress' house deep in the past. I asked her if she saw what transpired at the Ivory Wash. She said, "You were magnificent."

Tomorrow

This morning at 3:05 a.m. our Corgi woke me up moaning next to the bed. I patted him on the head and scratched his back but he didn't leave. He lay down next to the bed with his ears erect and his head pointed towards the bathroom. That is not normal behavior for him so I thought I should look around to see if anything was there in our bedroom.

Next to the settee there was a very large egg resting upright on its round end with the tapered end pointing straight up. It was almost five feet tall. The color was off-white. A slanted opening appeared in the side of the egg revealing a female person sitting inside on a little seat. She emerged from the egg and came over next to the bed close to me. She was very thin and tall. I estimated her height to be around six feet tall. She was wearing a floor length long sleeve silken gown that looked to me like an elaborate dressy nightgown.

I asked her several times who she was and why she was there. She continued to stare at me but never responded. I assumed that the egg was some kind of transport device so I got up and sat down inside of it. No sooner had I sat down than the egg closed shut and then opened after a few seconds. The egg was in the middle of an open space surrounded by tall grass and ground cover plants. I got out of the egg and saw a large futuristic structure about two hundred yards away. I followed the sloped walkway up to the structure and entered at its base. Inside there was what we would consider an elevator of some kind. It took me up to the top level, which was circular and saucer shaped with panoramic glass all around. It reminded me of the space needle but it was much more advanced technically. In the middle of this large circular room there was a single desk. Behind the desk there was a single large egg. The side of the egg opened and there was an elderly bearded man sitting inside the egg in front of the desk. His clothing was white as was his long beard. When I asked him where I was he said, "Tomorrow."

We engaged in a very long verbal exchange. He must have thought that I was really dense because I was not getting what he was trying to tell me. At first I thought he was talking about this place as being a part of our future. That was not the case. As it turned out 'Tomorrow' was the name of this place and it had nothing to do with our world or our future. It was not a different dimension. It was not an alternative reality. It was not a parallel universe. I had entered into a time system completely separate from our own. You might think of it as a time tunnel but the tunnel was immense like our own universe. You couldn't think of it as a parallel universe but perhaps as a completely separate universe. I had left our universe and entered into a different universe where time is present but not the same time as it is for us in our world and our universe.

After I returned to my bedroom there was a strong acidic smell that lasted several hours. It was a combination of acid and metal combined with the unmistakable smell of overheated electronic equipment.The Source had alluded to my leaving our time system and traveling along its surface outside of time to the distant past or distant future and then re-entering our time system to change something in the past or alter something in the future. I have been outside of our time system / universe in the past. It is extremely dangerous. It never occurred to me that I might enter into an alternative time system and travel through it into the past or into the future then exit that system and re-enter back into our own time system. That strategy might prove valuable and viable.

Working Wizards

The Source told me that having four wizards on Wizard Island created a functionable situation but that was not the same as a functional Wizard's Island. All four of the wizards had to be functioning in order for the full potential of the island to be realized.

This is what I had to work with: Jameson, the wizard on the lee side of the island, was a vegetarian. He was short and stocky. His outfit was something like St. Francis would wear. Samuel was the wizard on the left side of the lee. He was focused on making home brew. Clemson, the wizard on the right side of the lee was an isolationist. When I went to visit him recently he had created a huge defensive structure comprised of solid blocks of stone. These blocks were gigantic. I leveled the structure and told him to do something constructive with those huge stone blocks.

This is what I did. I had Jameson actively engage the Titans planting nutritional plants and vegetables on their fallow farmlands. He also showed them how to harvest, preserve and properly prepare them.

I had Samuel show the Titans how to make breads and pastries with the yeast from his home brewing activities as well how to ferment vegetables and make fine wines.

I had Clemson teach the Titans how to work with stone to create buildings and other architectural structures from native stone, which they quarried there on Wizard Island. All of these new skills gave meaning and purpose in the lives of the titans as well as the three other wizards. I continue to acquire those skill sets necessary to accomplish the specific tasks assigned to me by the Source.

Dr. Seuss

A few nights ago I went to visit Dr. Seuss for the first time. I was curious as to where he was and what he was doing. My old office was decorated throughout with his characters. Every March 2nd we would order a birthday cake and the staff would all gather around, light the candles and sing Happy Birthday to him. Then, we all ate cake.

Where I found him he was surrounded by all of the characters that he had created during his whole lifetime. They were real and life size. There was not a single human anywhere. I asked him about there not being any people there in his world. He said that this was heaven for him. He said that dealing with people had always been very problematic for him. I asked him if he were bothered by me being there in his world. Dr. Seuss replied, "Not at all. I gave you a big red clown nose, turned you into a kangaroo with one lop-ear hanging down and striped stockings on both of your feet and tail and two mittens that all were mismatched. You look just fine."

I told him that I had been tasked with convincing the Galactic Council not to terminate all human life on earth but I was having a very difficult time finding any redeeming qualities in all of humanity. Humans are killing everything and destroying the whole planet.

Apache Junction

Last night when I was talking with the Source I asked him what was next on his agenda for me to do. He said that he wanted me to go to Apache Junction.

When I was young we would drive through Apache Junction on our way to the lakes and trout streams in northern Arizona. There were two roads that crossed in the middle of the desert. That was Apache Junction. When I was little, I don't think there were even any stop signs just one road going north intersecting one road going east and west. When I was in college the roads were paved, had two lanes and a couple of stop signs that was it, no gas station, no houses, no people, only two roads crossing in the middle of nowhere. I could not even imagine what I was supposed to accomplish by going to Apache Junction.

When I got there they were having a pow-wow. There were lots of Indians everywhere. Some were decked out in traditional attire some were not. There were traditional drums and dancing as well as modern dancing and music. There was fry-bread and traditional as well as fast food concessions. There were pickups everywhere. They were mostly white Fords and Chevy models.

There was only one traditional tee-pee situated off to one edge of the pow-wow, with smoke trailing up out of the top opening where the supporting poles crossed and the flaps were pulled back for ventilation. I poked my head inside. There was total silence. Outside it was extremely noisy, inside not a single sound. One Indian man sat in front of the fire-pit located in the center of the tent dressed in a light tan buckskin outfit. His legs were crossed. He had a single eagle feather sticking straight up out of his headband. His long braided hair fell to one side of his weathered face. I assumed that he was a medicine man. I didn't stay long inside before I went back outside where the music was playing and there was food and dancing going on everywhere.

When I got back home I wondered what the point of going to Apache Junction had been. It couldn't have been for the music or the food or even the dancing. It must have had something to do with the medicine man in the tee-pee filled with its strange silence. So, I went back to the pow-wow in Apache Junction and back into that tee-pee. I sat down in front of the fire pit directly across from the medicine man facing him.

He took out his medicine pipe and lit it. He puffed on it several times and blew smoke over onto me. The smoke felt like acid eating away at my skin. I looked down at my body and I was a giant tooth being etched by acid before a new crown is placed down over it. I got up and left as fast as I could and returned home. The burning sensation subsided and I gave the whole experience some more thought. I still had no idea what the point of the experience had been but I knew that I needed to go back to Apache Junction again to try to find out.

When I returned to the pow-wow the medicine man was still sitting cross leg in front of the fire pit. I sat down directly across from him as he took out his medicine pipe again and began to puff on it. A large cloud of smoke billowed upwards in front of him and formed an Indian deer dancer that was in full costume complete with antlers and head mask. Then he handed his pipe to me.

I took the pipe from him in the traditional manner and began to puff on it. The smoke billowed up above the fire pit and became a great bear, a grizzly bear. The Indian deer dancer slowly dissipated and vanished into thin air but the grizzly bear became more and more real. It descended down upon me and I was transformed into a giant grizzly bear. The medicine man told me that I was to walk the earth from now on as a grizzly bear. For Native Americans the great grizzly bear has always been their spiritual protector here on earth.

I now understood what the importance was for me to go to Apache Junction. It is clear now what my future will be.

When I mentioned this to the Source he said, "... all my children are turning away from the light. Guide them back from darkness."

Styx

Last week when I was talking with the Source, he took me to the River Styx. I told him that I had been to the River Styx several times over the years. He said that he wanted me to have a better understanding of what the River Styx actually was. It is the separation between the world of the living and the Underworld. On the other side of the Styx there is Hell, Hades, the Underworld and the world of the undead. I always thought that Hell and Hades were different names for the same place but apparently that is not accurate. He further explained that Hell is the place of eternal damnation and has no connection with purgatory. Those that end up there are eternally damned. It is the domain of devils. Adjacent to Hell is Hades, which is a continuum of many levels and types of tortures all apparently in darkness. These are all connected to or with purgatory and as such there is the possibility of eventually getting out of there. It is the domain of Demons not Devils. Purgatory runs vertically up and down and is connected to Hades at a specific point.

Therefore, there are an infinite number of points at which an infinite number of purgatories can be attached to Hades, which runs horizontally. When you look straight out on the horizontal horizon that is where purgatory begins. It goes all the way down and attaches to Hades. An equally infinite number of heavens begins at the level of the horizon and extends upwards. All of these places exist outside of physical reality, as we know it.

Next to Hades is the Underworld, which has various degrees of darkness but it is not in total darkness. The Underworld may in fact not be connected to purgatory at all. The River Styx itself is filled with the undead. They are not dead and they are not alive but occupy the murky waters of the river itself. However, the undead are not the only occupants of the river by any means. They comprise only a minority of the inhabitants. The Source then said that the river is not actually water, as we know it but much, much more. Symbolically water is life and a river the living of life. It runs in both directions in some places but has a beginning and an end.

Arnott

(ar-nó)

Last night the Source asked me to go out to the island in the middle of the River Styx. I have been there before. It is a tiny island in name only because it is not more than six or seven feet in diameter and has a large rock on it. The island is located in a portion of the river that is more like a very large lake. When I have been there before some creature reaches up out of the murky water and grabs my ankle and tries to drag me down into the river. So, this time when I went to the Island I went as the giant grizzly bear. No sooner had I arrived than this thing emerged from the water. The first part that surfaced was the war helmet of a Trojan warrior. He was huge, close to seven feet tall and with his helmet on he was at least eight feet in total height. I, as a giant grizzly bear, stretched my powerful claws above his head to intimidate him but to my surprise he was totally covered in light colored tan clay and was completely blind. I got down on all four legs and he scrambled up onto my back because there was not room enough on the tiny island for both of us. I then proceeded to carry him the rest of the way across the river to the other side where the Underworld began. Upon reaching the other side of the river the clay, which incased his body fell away and he was no longer one of the undead but a new occupant of the underworld. He was very thankful for being rescued. He told me that his name was Arnott.

Hades

Hades is the Greek God of the dead and king of the Underworld. He is the brother of Zeus and Poseidon. The term Hades is also commonly used to refer to that part of the Underworld ruled by the God Hades.

The Source showed me the place on the other side of the river Styx where Hades resides. He told me that it is in complete darkness and is filled with demons as well as the dead. Purgatory is attached to it but it is vertical in orientation while Hades itself is laid out in a horizontal position like the rest of the Underworld. The Source asked me to go to Hades and learn as much as I could about it. He gave me a flat-bottomed disc with curved sides that emitted light that could be focused. It is protected by a razor-sharp circular blade, which protrudes if anyone ties to grab it. The inhabitants of Hades cannot stand light. It causes them great pain. The Source said that this light-emitting disc would protect me from harm while I was in Hades.

He suggested that I first go to Hades as a pinpoint awareness and position myself as two points of awareness, one on either shoulder of Hades the God. He said that I would have to adapt to the complete darkness by using my wizard's powers of observation to see things even in the absence of any light. I tried this approach for three hours without any success.

Brothers...Two

The next night I returned and positioned myself on both of Hades' shoulders and remained there for about forty-five minutes. By the end of that period I was just beginning to be able to see things very close by. I returned home and took a break. I never believed that there was a God Hades. I always thought that there was no truth to mythology. I reasoned if there were a God Hades then there must also be his two brothers Zeus and Poseidon. So, I went to visit the God Zeus and sure enough he also exists. I went attired only in the leather thong given to me by Aru, the keeper of Dream Time.

When I arrived I introduced myself and told Zeus that I had just visited his brother Hades and wanted to also meet his two brothers. Zeus was very considerate and polite and seemed to understand my motivation for self-introduction. From there I proceeded to where Poseidon was located.

Poseidon was not as open to my self-introduction as his brother Zeus. He wanted to know what it was that I wanted from him. I told Poseidon that I did not seek any favors from him. I told him that if I asked something of him then he would ask something of me in return. He extended his jade drinking vessel towards me and as I reached out to accept it he dropped it and it shattered into pieces. I instinctively stopped time and replayed the event only this time I anticipated his ploy and snatched his stone cup out of thin air as he released it. I placed it at his feet. He was truly shocked by what had just transpired before his very eyes. He said, "It was foretold that a human would someday come who could do things that the Gods could not do. His name will be Mikel. What is your name?"

I am Michael and I can do many things.

He said, "Show me!" So I became the White Wizard. Then I became a giant White Wizard. Then I became the great Grizzly Bear. Then I became a giant Grizzly Bear, much larger than Poseidon himself. Then I just vanished into thin air.

When I returned home I shared my experience with the Source. He told me that the Gods were very powerful but the one advantage I had over them was that I could manipulate time and they could not. They were prisoners of time itself and I was not.

The Source wanted me to continue working on being able to see in Hades without the benefit of light and to also find the three-headed dog Cerberus and to also locate the three Furies, the three goddesses of vengeance.

I, Claudius

I went to Hades several times before I mastered the art of seeing where there was complete darkness. It was challenging but once I got the hang of it the process became almost automatic. The field of vision was copper-tone in appearance. I don't know what made it that way but I could definitely see quite clearly. I located the three headed dog which was on the other side of Hades guarding the official entrance way. Instead of two separate points of awareness I became three points, one on top of each of the dog's heads. Then I became four points of awareness so that

I could observe the three heads of the dogs from an alternative point of view.

When I returned home it was almost two o'clock in the morning so I went out to catch the night bus. The night bus was waiting for me when I got there with its doors wide open. I jumped inside and asked Brad, the bus driver what he was hauling tonight. He said that he had a load of Fools. I asked how he determined that someone was a fool. He gave me his definition of what constituted a fool and I asked where he was taking them. He told me to Fool Island. I asked if this load of fools were dead or alive. He said that some of them were dead but most of them were still alive. I asked how long they would be there and he told me until they recognized that they were fools and stopped doing foolish things. I jumped at the chance and asked if he could stop on his way and pick up a fool that I knew personally and take her to the island in hopes that all of the foolish things that these fools would be doing might convince her of how foolish she was acting. The bus driver took a detour and in a few minutes we were on our way to Fool Island with this foolish woman I know, going along for the ride. When we arrived at the island the front of the bus tilted up in the air and we all were dumped out onto the ground on Fool Island.

I felt that this was no place for me and tried to make my way back home. I ended up in the presence of a Roman emperor deep in the past. I bowed before him in a gesture of respect since I was just passing through on my way back to my own time. He took personal offense at my gesture and commanded me, "Kneel before me, I am Claudius. I am the emperor."

I transformed into a giant Grizzly Bear and raised my paws high above his head in a very threatening manner and then I transformed into a wizard and said, "I am Michael the White Wizard of the South." I made myself twelve feet tall and then vanished into my own time. I plan on returning to Fool Island periodically to see if the lady's experience there helped her to stop acting so foolishly all the time.

The Taskmaster

On Friday the 22nd of December Stephen died from a drug overdose. He was forty-three years old. That does not bode well for him. We were in Orange County visiting for the Christmas holidays. I went looking for Stephen early on the morning of the twenty-fourth of December. I found him sitting on the curb in front of his parent's house. He was still completely wasted so I took him into their house and dumped him on a bed and left him there to sober up. He of course had no idea that he was dead.

Late that evening, on Christmas Eve, my wife and I were sitting on the sofa in front of the fireplace in the living room. My wife was watching the fire and I was reading a book to my Granddaughter. My wife said to me that she just saw someone walk past her into the family room. Later she elaborated on what she had seen. She said that she saw a woman walk by her out of the corner of her eye. The woman was wearing a black, floor-length, hooded robe that covered her face.

Later after everyone had retired for the evening, I went looking for this hooded woman. It didn't take me too long to find her. I asked her if she were death. She said that she wasn't death but an assistant who had been sent to gather up Stephen and take him to the 'Taskmaster' to be given appropriate punishment. That didn't sound too encouraging to me. I asked to see her face. She was a skeleton. I asked her why she was here bothering me. She said that when she went looking for Stephen, he was nowhere to be found, so she followed my trail from his parent's house to where I was staying there in California.

I told her that I needed to talk with her supervisor. Maybe we could cut a deal with respect to Stephen's proscribed punishment. Her supervisor turned out to be an assistant taskmaster and he had no authority to make any deals whatsoever. So, from there we went to the see the Taskmaster. He was dressed all in black and was sitting at a small desk engrossed in his paper work. I asked the Taskmaster about cutting some deal on Stephen's behalf. He insisted that he had to follow protocol and could not deviate from the proscribed punishment. Only the 'Assignment Angel' could alter that punishment. I said, "Well, let's go then to see the Assignment Angel." All three of them went with me.

I have had several encounters with the Assignment

Angel. She is never happy to see me. She told me that Stephen was not supposed to die for twenty-five years so something would have to be done with him until then. His case was not being assessed strictly as a suicide but he had to be punished for his contribution to his own early demise. She said I needed to have an acceptable alternative proposal otherwise; the Task-master would punish him as customary. We all left the assignment Angel together. I went back to California to come up with some acceptable plan.

What I came up with was to have Stephen spend the next twenty-five years in the cave with the Buddha of the Mountain. I visited the Buddha first to make sure it was acceptable to him before I asked Death's Assistant to share my plan with the Assignment Angel and get her approval. When she returned with the authorization from the Assignment Angel's approval parts of her face were covered in flesh.

The next challenge for me was to locate Stephen. I finally found him wandering the streets of the red light district in Bangkok, Thailand. I grabbed him by the scruff of his neck and we transported together into the Buddha's cave, where I informed him that he was dead and that he had to stay there meditating for twenty-five years. After that, the Assignment Angel would assign him to his next life. The alternative was to be severely punished by the Taskmaster.

When Death's assistant and I went together to tell the Assignment Angel that Stephen was now with the Buddha, the Assignment Angel fleshed out the face of death's assistant and gave her the scroll for her next life. She vanished as she accepted the scroll. The Assignment Angel gave me a frown and then she also disappeared leaving me alone in what always reminds me of the Bonneville Salt Flats.

Entrapment

After a busy night of other pursuits I chose to venture back in time and place to once again visit with the Oracle in his cave. It was dark inside. Darker than usual, even black as ink I suppose. I have forgotten how dark true darkness can seem to be since now I have acquired the power to see quite well even in the absolute absence of light. I echoed my arrival into the darkness of his cave but there was no response.

After thoroughly searching his cave to discover no one there, I expanded my endeavor to the area around the entrance to the cave and on up the trail to the flatland above. In larger circles, I spiraled around and around covering ever-larger areas. Only after much searching did I finally come upon his body lying cold and stiff on the wind swept plain.

I had forgotten how old and frail he has become. His weight seemed less burdensome some how in my quest to move him back into the safety of his cave below. Once in there I summoned Simon, the Ship's Surgeon and Edgar Casey, the psychic healer, to assist me in my efforts to revive the Oracle. He was cold to the touch with thready pulse, shallow respiration and non-responsive. He had three small gumdrop shaped muffins or cupcakes stuck to his forehead. I pried them off and soaked them in spring water from inside his cave, then forced them down his throat with a small spoon. Nothing seemed to arouse him from his coma-tose-like condition. Both the Ship's Surgeon and the psychic healer said that his body was still clinging to life but his spirit was absent. Someone had entrapped his awareness. We wrapped him in warm blankets and did everything we could to assist him but Simon and Edgar Casey said that without the return of his aware-ness his body would soon die.

I extended my awareness out in every direction as far as I could but came up with nothing. I tried every-thing that I could think of but nothing seemed to work. Then, I remembered that silver thread that connects our awareness to our own bodies until the moment of our death. I located this tiny thread and followed it for hundreds of miles through hills and mountains, forests and streams until I finally located the Oracle's aware-ness contained in a glass sphere hidden in a tiny cabin in the midst of a dense forest high up in the mountains. Someone or something had captured the awareness of the Oracle and imprisoned it in a thick glass ball.

The thin iridescent thread was wrapped around a small wooden spool many, many times before it en-tered the glass, globe-like wire on an electromagnet. I suspected this was some kind of trap with the Oracle being used as bait.

Damian

The Source insisted that I return again and again to Hades each time with specific additional tasks for me to accomplish. This has been on going now for a couple of weeks. I eventually was able to locate the three Furies. They were located on a tiny island situated in the middle of a very wide part of the river Styx. The Furies are the three goddesses of vengeance. Tisiphone is the avenger of murder, Megaera is for jealousy and Alecto is for constant anger. They are the daughters of Uranus and Gaea.

Hades was supposed to be filled with demons but I was unable to locate a single one. After much effort I finally acquired the ability to see these demons but that required the ability to process a different form of non-light vision. Purgatory was also supposed to be attached to Hades but again I was unable to visualize it until I mastered a third form of non-light sight.

I eventually located a woman frozen in Purgatory like in the movie Ground Hog's Day where everything was repeated over and over every day for her. It was a bizarre experience for me. She had been there since committing suicide in the year 1917 when she was informed that her fiancée was killed in the 1st World War. She jumped off of a bridge. Her name was Nancy and she was six months pregnant at the time of her death. It took me awhile but I managed to free her up and get her on the way to resolution. As she began to make progress she began moving upward in an expanding transparent tube of some sort. The Source wanted me to get someone out of Purgatory as my next assignment.

I took a short cut and figured out how to extricate Nancy since she had already done her time there and had momentum and was moving rapidly up out of Purgatory on her own. Once I got her out of Purgatory I put her in a safe place temporarily. This did not sit well with the Source who wanted me to understand the process required of extrication more completely.

I discovered that each individual was inside a transparent tube. There were several tiny threads attached to them like spider webs. If I touched one of these threads demons quickly responded. I needed to figure out a way to work around this alarm system.

For my next rescue I chose a giant creature that was on the surface of Hades and not inside of a tube. He was big and ugly and had a thick steel collar around his neck that was anchored down by a heavy chain to a cement pier. I stopped time and put a bubble of time around both of us then I severed the chain and we floated up to the surface and out of Purgatory.

I asked who and what he was. He said that his name was Damian and he was a demon. He told me that everyone hated him for all the bad things he always did. I told him that I was his friend. I had set him free and he could travel with me on my many adventures but from now on he could only do good things. He agreed to those conditions and I removed the heavy steel collar from around his neck and took him to the same safe place where I had taken Nancy and introduced him to the inhabitants there as their protector.

Five Rivers

The Source showed me the five rivers that surround Hades. The river Styx separates our world from the world of the dead. To its left is the river of fire, which separates Hades from Hell. It is known as the river Phlegethon. On the right side is the river of light, which separates Hades from the rest of the Underworld. If you approach Hades from its opposite side where the official entrance to Hades is located that is guarded by the three-headed dog, the abyss would be to your right. I think the river Cocytus, the river of woe, may be located there but I'm not sure. To your left is some kind of conveyor system that comprises that river. It flows along the border of Hades. That river could be the Archeron, the river of lamentation or it could be the Lethe, the river of forgetfulness. The Source told me that I was not yet ready to encounter those two rivers.

While we were discussing the five rivers that surround Hades, I asked about the conundrum for me of the river Styx emerging from the ground, as it were, at its source and nearby re-entering the ground. That was an unresolved issue for me. The Source said that the river Styx did in fact re-enter the subterranean world very near its point of origin. He said that what

I assumed was an island in the middle of the Styx where the three Furies resided was in fact surrounded by the river Styx on almost all of its perimeter with the river flowing in one direction on one side and the opposite direction on the other side. The river Styx was joined by the river Acheron, before it turned back and re-entered the subterranean world near its point of origin. I asked about Hades being encircled seven times by the river Styx and the Source said that was not the case but the elaborate layout of the five rivers plus the Styx doubling back on itself in two places might give that impression. In some places the Styx is very wide like a lake and other places very narrow like a stream. None of the five rivers are in fact rivers as we know rivers but for our minds the concept 'river' most closely conveys some of their qualities.

The Source not only insists that I have a functional understanding of Hades and Purgatory but that I also need to be functionally competent in working within the rest of what comprises the 'Underworld' before I am considered a fully functioning wizard and am no longer considered a wizardling.

Frankfurter

When I woke up last night I checked the clock to see what time it was. The clock sits on my nightstand about ten inches away from my face. The numerals are bright red and about an inch high. It displayed

1:58 a.m. I jumped up and ran outside to catch the night bus at 2:00 o'clock. The old bus wobbled from side to side as it rounded the corner. Maybe it needs new shock absorbers. The tires were squished down like they were low on air or carrying a very heavy load. I climbed on board and asked Brad the raccoon bus driver what he was hauling tonight. He told me, 'frankfurters'. I of course asked where he had gotten so many wieners. He told me they were all outdated and he had to dispose of them. I told Brad that I needed to go to the 'Underworld' because I had been going to Hades for sometime now and it was time for me to get on with this project.

We floated up a bit in the old school bus before it took a nosedive and we ended up in what supposedly was the 'Underworld'. The bus came to a stop several feet above the surface. It tilted nose up and the back of the bus sprung open and all of the frankfurters poured out into a pile with me on top. It vanished and I was alone in this poorly illuminated place. I could see but it was really dim compared to the light intensity on the surface of earth. The characters that I saw there I would have to describe as a cross between chimpan- zees and humans. One came up to me and asked what this big pile of stuff was. I told him or her they were frankfurters, hot dogs, wieners but they were obviously not familiar with them. I told them that they were made from meat and they were to eat. The creature asked if they could have one. I told them they could have them all. The pile was immediately surrounded by about a dozen of these creatures. A line formed behind each one and they began passing the frankfurters along from hand to hand as fast as they could until all of the wieners were gone.

The character I had been conversing with told me that they were meat eaters and only ate meat. I looked all around and then asked them from where they got their meat. They said, pointing up at the sky, "From above". While we were talking a group of about sixteen large specimens of these creatures came by. They were harnessed together in two columns pulling a carriage with a fat dignitary sitting inside. I took the liberty and disintegrated the harness restraining them. The indentured chimps ran off in every direction leaving the dignitary shaking his fist at them, fruitlessly in the air. I returned to my home and checked the time again. It read 1:44 a.m. That was sixteen minutes before I had left in the first place. It didn't make any sense to me as to how that could be correct so I asked the Source. He said that time in the Underworld was not the same as our time. There time went in the other direction in some parts and in other parts there was no time at all.

Tornado

Last night, at 1:56 a.m., I received a text message on my phone from my son in California. It read, "Tornado here, come check it out."

So, I immediately transported over to his house. In

the family room there was indeed a tornado whirling around in a clockwise direction. There were all kinds of things being sucked up and scattered around. I had never encountered anything like it before. It always reminded me of a dust devil which are common in the southwest desert in the summer time. When I was a child we would always try to chase the whirlwinds down to get inside of them. That was quite an experience. But, I wasn't about to get inside this dust devil because I had no idea what it was, what it could do or where it came from.

I asked Iky who was watching it from across the room if he had anything to do with this crazy tornado thing. He knew nothing about it. I didn't know what to do with it so I surrounded it with the magic leather pouch of suspended animation, which I always carry with me. After investigating this thing I learned that it was indeed a thing and that it was attracted to places where there was conflict. This 'Tornado' fed on conflict and in the process created chaos.

For now it was safely constrained within the pouch of suspended animation. But I have no idea what I should do with it.

Poseidon

I had gone to sit on the park bench overlooking the Event Horizon and visit with the Facilitator and Sabatini. I noticed some disturbance far out on the sea of the Event Horizon. I asked if anyone wanted to accompany me when I went to investigate the disturbance. No one was interested so I went on my own. When I reached the area above the disturbance I sank down to the bottom of the sea looking for its source. I ended up next to Poseidon. He wanted to know what was creating the problem. I told him that the disturbance was probably created by aliens. This certainly got his attention. I managed to convince him that aliens were planning on terminating human life on earth. I also told him that I could take him to where the Galactic Council convened if he wanted me to. He was eager to go with me. I didn't want him grabbing onto my arm or some other part of my body. So I grabbed his trident and asked him to hold on to it as well. That way we wouldn't get separated on the journey.

When we arrived I introduced Poseidon to the Galactic Council and reminded them that although we had a non-aggression pact with each other, Poseidon did not have such a pact with them and if they did anything to any other humans, Poseidon, who was a God, would deal with them very harshly.

Correlations

Supposedly there are twenty-six correlations in total. Our world and our reality are comprised of only seven specific correlations. Anything that has those specific seven correlations in the correct amounts and specific relationships to each other exists on earth. I don't know what those specific seven correlations are but my guess is that they involve Time as well as spatial qualities like Density, Duration, Frequency, Synchronicity, Sensitivity and Intent. Other possible correlations that come to my mind are things like: Continuity, Fragmentation, Loci, Dimensions, Realities, Destination, Direction of Flow, Velocity, Perceptibility, Probability, Possibility, Trajectory, Energy content, Matter, Antimatter, Dark matter, Gravity, Antigravity, Different Universes, Good, Evil, Location of travel i.e. Inside or outside of time tubes, as well as which particular tube the entity is traveling in.

The Source and I had a long and detail-filled encounter last night. He insisted that I have a basic appreciation and familiarity with many of the realms that I could encounter as a wizard.

The Source built his explanation in spatial terms even though space is essentially irrelevant. He began with the horizon as a reference point, not a curved horizon like the curvature of the earth but a horizontal line extending in either direction indefinitely. That which falls below the surface of the horizon is loosely referred to as the 'Underworld'. Those areas close to and parallel with the surface of the earth either above or below its surface are the Astral planes where people can engage in Astral-projection. Below these astral planes lies the Underworld. It is comprised of Hell on the far left, which is inhabited by Devils and is the place of eternal damnation and is the realm of infinite impossibility.

Next to it is Hades. It is separated from Hell by the 'River of Fire' on its left border and from the rest of the Underworld per say by the river of Light on its right side. Hades is the realm of the God Hades. It is populated with Demons and is the realm of eternal darkness. Hades is separated from earth by the river Styx. It is separated on the other side by two rivers. The entrance into Hades is guarded by 'Cerberus', the three-headed dog. It is situated between the river of darkness on the left (Acheron) as viewed from our side of Hades and the river of forgetfulness on the right side, which is known as the river Lethe. The three Furies reside in Hades, as does the three-headed dog 'Cerberus'. I have had encounters with the three Furies, Alecto, (Unceasing anger), Tisphone, (Avenger of Murder) & Megaera, (Jealousy) as well as with the three-headed dog.

Purgatory is located directly above Hades and is tended by Demons but it is not actually a part of Hades but is oriented vertically above it.

Paradise and Heaven are located above the astral planes. Paradise is concave and has a bowl like configuration. Heaven is at the far end of paradise and is vertical in orientation. Heaven is the place of eternal light and infinite possibilities. It is populated with pure disembodied spirits. There are no human forms there. Human forms populate paradise but not heaven.

Gutman

Jonathan passed unexpectedly a week ago. His untimely death concerned me. I wanted to check on him and see how he was managing his new situation. I had no idea where he was but I felt it would be less problematic for him if I went to where he was instead of having him come to where I was. When I located him he was walking with another man who was wearing a brown, hooded, floor length cloak. Jonathan was wearing casual clothes and was carrying a backpack. They were walking briskly along a dirt pathway in the middle of a desert wilderness. I walked behind them having difficulty keeping up with their rapid pace. I attempted to communicate with Jonathan several times to no avail, before I tapped him on the shoulder to get his attention. I asked where they were going and why they were walking so fast. He said that they were in a hurry because they were late. But he never told me why he was late or where he was headed. When I tapped the other man on his shoulder to get his attention, he vanished. I asked Jonathan what the fellow traveler's name was and he said, "Job".

I asked Jonathan if he wanted to take a break and we sat down on a rock near the trail we were walking on. There was a stream not to far down the hill below us and so I asked him if he saw the stream or small river. He said that he did and then I asked what he was carrying in his backpack. He said that he didn't know what was in the backpack. I asked if he knew where he was but he didn't know. I asked how long it had been since he last ate and he didn't remember. I asked what the last thing he ate was and after much deliberation he said that he had eaten chicken but that it didn't agree with his stomach and that was the last thing he remembered. He didn't know what day it was or where he was going or why he was in such a hurry.

I suggested that he look inside of his backpack and see what he was carrying.

He opened it up and the first thing he removed from the backpack was a large egg. It wasn't a chicken egg because it was much larger than a chicken egg. It was so large that I thought it could be a duck egg or maybe even a goose egg. The second thing he removed was a round rock slightly larger than the egg. The third thing he removed from his backpack was a baseball. The next thing was a stick a little over a foot in length and about ¾ of an inch in diameter. The last thing he removed was a hand full of feathers. They weren't chicken feathers but gray feathers from a pigeon or a morning dove. We talked at length about what those things represented in general and to him specifically.

Jonathan struggled to give meaning to those items he had been carrying in his backpack. I felt they were critical for him to understanding his current situation. For me the egg represented a new beginning, like Easter and spring represents rebirth and new life. The rock represents something hard, something heavy and something enduring like life and death itself. Baseball represents a game, the game of life. A stick is part of a tree that was once part of a living tree but is now no longer alive. The stick represents his piece of the tree of life and part of his own family tree. Dove feathers represent peace and hope but the dove itself is now gone. The person who accompanied him on his journey through the wilderness was Job a biblical prophet. The wilderness itself also alludes to the biblical journey of redemption. And the river down below where we were sitting was in fact the river Jordan. I explained this to Jonathan and suggested that he toss all those things he was carrying into the river and then get on with it.

He wanted me to toss the items into the river but I told him that this was his journey and his task not mine. Jonathan said that he liked the egg and wanted to toss it into the river last of all.

First he tossed the rock into the river as he stood on an outcropping. The stone sank to the bottom of the stream and was transformed into gold. The second thing he tossed into the water was the baseball. It turned into a small wooden boat and drifted away down the river. I asked which way it drifted, to the right with the current or to the left against the current. He said that it drifted with the current down the river to the right. I asked him to look up the river to the left and tell me what he saw. He saw that same little wooden boat drifting towards him from his left, and passing by heading to his right. Every minute or so, the boat would drift by once again continuing on its journey. Next he dropped the stick into the water. It sank straight to the bottom as if it were made of iron.

After the stick Jonathan dumped the pile of feathers into the river and the river turned a beautiful blue like the color of a tropical sea. Before he dropped the egg into the water he threw his backpack into the river. It unraveled and became a bundle of threads waving in the current stretching off into the distance attached to the spot where the backpack entered the river. The last thing he tossed into the river was the oversized egg. It sank immediately to the bottom of the river and all of the things he had tossed into the river began to coalesce around the egg and up out of the water popped a white swan with its prominent black bill. It grew larger and larger as Jonathan shrank smaller and smaller. When the swan was full size Jonathan was as small as a hamster. I picked him up, dunked him into the river Jordan and placed him on the back of the swan. I told him to hold onto the swan's neck by wrapping his arms and legs around the swan's neck. They flew away together. The magical white swan was transporting Jonathan Gutman off to begin his next life.

My assessment was that this was his purgatory. There is no way to know how long Jonathan would have wandered in the desert wilderness before he figured out that he was deceased and how to extricate himself from this place. It could have been a very long time. I in essence short-circuited his stay here in Purgatory. I liked Jonathan. He was a good man.

Itsacono

Sharing this experience is intended only to expand the arena of possibility for you. I was awake and in bed when images about six inches square began to appear in my field of vision. These images were the same with my eyes open or with them closed. An image would form then some parts of it would animate and then that image would be replaced by another image emerging from the right side of my field of vision and exiting to the left side of my field of vision. It was almost like a slide show. This process continued for a long time. I was trying to figure out how this process was possible. The images appeared to be elaborate etchings or engravings to be used to illustrate books or papers from a long time ago before there were any photographs available. The content appeared to be from the fourteenth or fifteenth century based on the subjects and the subject matter. I don't know what they were supposed to refer to. While focused on this process a scene from a dense jungle momentarily appeared. Between the leaves I saw part of a face staring out at me. It was the left eye and cheek of a person. I noticed the glint in the eye as well as the white sclera when the eye moved. It appeared to me to be the face of an Inca Indian. Their faces are unique. I didn't know for sure if it were the face of a female or of a younger male but I was determined to find that person.

It took a while but I located him in the jungle deep in the past. I presented myself in a small clearing in the jungle as an Aborigine dressed only in a leather thong given to me by Aru the keeper of Dream Time. As he circled around me I moved to face him as though I were standing on a turntable. Communication was clear and precise though neither he nor I moved our lips. Communication must have been telepathic. He told me that his mother's dying wish was for him to find the Sorcerer who had rescued her and his warrior father from certain death.

I asked if she were still alive. He said that she was. He took me to her. She was lying in her bed waiting for death to take her. She had cataracts and was blind. I magically removed her cataracts and she could see once again but she didn't recognize me in my present form as an Aborigine. I told her that I was a shape shifter and transformed myself back into a familiar form. Because she could now see once again she resumed her daily activities and I departed back into my own time.

I asked the Source how that whole process could have transpired and how the Inca Prince could have located me far in the future. He said that we must have some history. We must have some connection. I wondered if he possibly could have been a prior incarnation of myself. To test this hypothesis I went to the edge of the abyss and crossed over on the 'Wizard's Bridge'. On the other side of the abyss standing on the right side of that end of the bridge are all of my former incarnations. The Inca Prince was there among them. He was a former incarnation of myself. The

Source told me some time ago that I must locate each of my past and future incarnations and meld with them before I would be complete. I put the Inca Prince on like you would put on a Hawaiian shirt and then went through the 'Door of No Return' and we were one. I had gone back in time and saved the Inca Princess and her warrior guard who became the parents of the Inca Prince who summoned me from the future at his mother's request. Itsacono the Inca prince is a prior incarnation of myself.

e-land

The Source reminded me that I needed to re-establish connections with my other life experiences. So I returned to the edge of the abyss and crossed over the Wizard's bridge to the other side.

Just to the right of the other end of the bridge all of my past lives were milling around. I asked if any of them wished to join me for an adventure. None of them were receptive to that idea. Then as if by magic, I started to rise up into the air as if I were on an invisible elevator. At what I would guess was five or six stories up a young man in his late twenties appeared in a doorway. He came out to greet me. He told me his name was e-land. I asked if his name were Elon but he repeated his name and then spelled it for me, e-land. I asked if he were the person that I communicated with from the future on my computer. He said that he was and that he was a future incarnation of myself. I asked if he would be willing to go on an adventure with me. The Source wanted me to get any of my past lives who were willing to go with me to return to the event horizon for some unspecified challenge. I didn't want e-land to get lost so I grab onto his wrists and he grabbed onto mine and we returned to the park bench on the island where Sabatini, the Facilitator and the young boy Lucky were sitting. I asked them if anyone there wanted to go with us out onto the event horizon. Much to my surprise all three of them wanted to go along with e-land and myself. The Facilitator and Sabatini joined in the wristlock arrangement and Lucky climbed up on top of our interlocked wrists and joined in the adventure. We drifted out across the waters until we reached a spot where there was a disturbance down below us in the water. There we sank down to where the disturbance was located. We were engulfed within a large air bubble. e-land escorted us through a doorway into what appeared to me to be an eight-sided room. When I asked him about the shape of the room e-land said that it was actually ten-sided. The place reminded me of a control tower at an airport with high plate glass windows that sloped inward at the bottom. All around him were these wispy ghost-like people that e-land said were actually people who existed sometime in the future. He took me over to a small white mushroom desk with a single, pedestal-shaped support where he began to activate different functions. All of the ghostlike images disappeared. I

224

floated up to the surface of the water and made my way back to the park bench and sat down on it. The Facilitator, Sabatini and the young boy Lucky were all gone. After a short time, the Oracle materialized and sat down next to me on the bench and then e-land materialized and sat down on my right side. I clasped right hands with the Oracle and left hands with e-land like we were shaking hands. The Oracle said, "You are the connection between past and future events."

My World

Last night, when I was in 'The Place' recovering from another adventure, the Source said, "Walk with me.' Where we were walking there was nothing. We came upon a white wooden fence about thirty-eight inches high. It was solid, not a picket fence, the top was flat and four or five inches thick. We stopped at the fence, which was solid with no gate anywhere. The Source asked me what I saw on the other side of the fence. On this side of the fence there was nothing, a total lack of anything. Even the surface we were walking on was not visible. Everything was just black.

On the other side of the fence there was also nothing but that nothingness wasn't black. It was more like dust on a windy day but there was nothing that I could discern but it was quite different from the side of the fence we were standing on. The Source told me that the side we were standing on was completely without anything. It wasn't the 'void' and it wasn't 'emptiness'. There just wasn't anything anywhere on that side of the fence. He opened an invisible gate in the fence and it swung open. Not outward towards us but inward. He told me to walk through the gate. So, I did. The arc created by the gate opening had a semicircle of gray cement. As I stepped off of the cement to close the gate, a square of grass appeared where I stepped. The Source asked me to return to the other side so I did. When I closed the gate it disappeared and the white wooden wall was once again a solid fence.

The Source asked me to tell him what I saw when I was on the other side. I told him. Then the Source told me that on the other side of the fence was 'Your world.' He elaborated and said that I could choose to enter that world now or later or never. That was entirely up to me. But, in order for me to claim it I had to name it or otherwise I would never be able to find it again. He also said that everything in that world would be of my own creation.

My first thought was to name it 'tomorrow land'.

He said, "Tomorrow never comes."

Then I settled on 'My World" for its name. The Source then asked when I wanted to go there. I said, "There is no time like now". So I walked through the gate and when I closed it the fence disappeared entirely leaving me in a world of my own making where the only things there would be things of my own creation.

Reunion

I woke up this morning at two o'clock and rushed outside to see if the Night Bus was still there. It was waiting for me in the street with its doors wide open. As I jumped on board I asked the bus driver where he was headed tonight. He said, "To the reunion." I asked, "What reunion". He responded, "Your reunion."

I looked back at the passengers on the bus. It was filled with my past lives. The bus bounced along for a while before it stopped in an open field of green grass. I was the first one off of the bus. I greeted each of the passengers as they departed from the bus and shook hands with them. After the last passenger got off of the bus, it vanished. When I turned around all of the passengers were gone. The field of green grass was now punctuated by rows of flat gravestones. There was one for each of my past lives.

I wondered if my past lives were still on the other side of Wizard's bridge so I went there and checked. There was no one there. I had been re-united with each of my past lives when I greeted each of them and shook hands with them as they passed by to their final resting places in the "green field aplenty".

The Garden

I was in 'The Place' recharging from time travel.

The Source asked me to walk with him. He asked me what I saw. I told him that we were surrounded by all kinds of beautiful flowers. It was very green and lush but not like a jungle because we were walking on a wide manicured path of some sort. The Source said that this was 'The Garden'. He asked me to describe the path we were walking on. It wasn't hard and it wasn't soft and squishy. It wasn't gravel or sand or anything crunchy. It was almost like walking on a cloud. It was certainly unlike anything I have ever walked on before.

The Source told me that the plants that made up the garden consisted of all of the different flowering plants that have ever existed on planet earth even those that are now extinct. He said that the garden was actually spherical in shape with different sections having different kinds of plants. There was a section for conifers another for deciduous trees, one for cycads and so forth. He said that as new plants were created they drifted down the stream of time and accumulated here in the garden like a dam blocks a stream and everything that the stream is carrying accumulates in the pond or lake created by the dam.

He said that the path we were walking on was actually that stream of time and the stream accumulated inside of the sphere created by the spherical layer of plants. This then was a repository not only for plants but also for time itself. This is where I could come to gather time if I should need some. He wanted me to know where to find time and to learn how to dispense it.

Buddha on the mountain

Last night I went to 'The Place' to recharge my energy supplies. I was talking with the Source when I mentioned to him that I felt like I needed to visit the Buddha on the mountain. The Source told me that if I felt like going to see the Buddha then I probably needed to go there for some reason. So, when I left 'The Place' I went to see the Buddha on the mountain.

He lives in a tiny cave far up on the side of an ice-covered mountain that has no trail or path leading to it. He is always sitting in a hollowed-out alcove at the end of his cave meditating in front of his stone fire pit with his eyelids almost completely closed.

As soon as I entered his cave, the Buddha said to me, "Michael leave your troubles at the door". His cave doesn't even have a door. I went back outside and sat down for a few minutes before returning. The Buddha again told me to leave my troubles at the door. This process was repeated several times before I was invited to sit on the other side of the fire pit and talk with the Buddha. When I was ready to leave, the Buddha said, "You cannot change the world. You can change yourself. When you change yourself, your world will change."

I returned later and asked the Buddha if I could bring another person there to see him. He said,

"Think about what you just asked Michael. How

long did it take you to acquire the skills necessary to make your way here to my cave? Each person must find their own way."

Leopards four

My son sent a text message last night while we were watching "The Man Who Knew Infinity", which is a movie about Srinivasa Ramanujan the famous mathematician from India. His text read: "Small, black panther here." I paused the movie and returned his text: "Where is it?"He said that it was in the living room. I replied, "I will come for it later."

I wasn't sure how best to proceed. I finally decided to go over as a pure-point awareness. When I did so I discovered that there were two small black panthers in his living room as well as two large adult black panthers, the mother and the father of the two cubs. I didn't know why they were there or what I should do with them but I couldn't just leave them there in my son's living room.

Eventually I discovered why they were there and what was needed to get them on their way. I must admit that I am a little slow on the draw sometimes. Apparently there is a rift that runs through my son's house starting out near the street and extending all the way to the back yard back next to the pool house. They were in transit from one dimension into another dimension. I had recently stationed a very large giant in the pool house leaving him with specific instructions to protect my son's house from all intruders without realizing that his house was in fact a transit point for other creatures. The family of four black panthers needed only safe passage and they were back on their way.

When I mentioned this encounter with the panthers to the Source, I asked him how I would know when I am no longer a mere wizardling. He said, "When you are a wizard" and he disappeared into a dense fog bank. It has been raining for three days and three nights and the clouds were down to ground level, which is a rare happening in the desert southwest that is plagued by longstanding drought.

The gauge

Last night I went to 'The Place' to recharge my energy supply. While I was there the Source reminded me that the energy available in this place was infinite but I had no way to determine how much energy I had or how much energy I needed. He presented me with a 'Heads up display' that he referred to as a 'gauge'. Sure enough in the lower right hand side of my field of vision a small round gauge appeared. It was similar in appearance to that of an old fashion gas gauge from an automobile with one modification. The dial on the face of the gauge was circular like a clock rather than being an arc like on a car. It registered at more than half full. The Source said that with the aid of the energy gauge I could control the rate at which my energy supply was refilled and by monitoring the movement of the gauge I was able to fully recharge in two seconds without overcharging, which would have been disastrous. The Source also informed me that neither the Oracle or e-land had any way to restore the energies that they used during their non-ordinary endeavors but it was possible for me to recharge them through personal contact. So I took leave immediately and went to the Event Horizon to meet up with the two of them.

In the past the Oracle sat on my left side and e-land sat on my right side. I crossed my arms and held right hands with the Oracle and left hands with e-land. This time when the two of them sat down next to me on the park bench that overlooked the Event Horizon, I extended my left hand to the Oracle on my left side and my right hand to e-land on my right side resulting in them having their arms across their body and my arms being spread wide open. I was holding hands respectively with each of them in a handshake. This allowed for an immediate transfer of energy to both.

As that occurred I stood up and began to walk out over the waters of the Event Horizon further and further until I had passed completely over the events unfolding beneath my feet and arrived at another small sandy island with its own park bench facing back towards where I had come from. I turned around and looked back across the sea of water that constituted the Event Horizon as I sat down on the park bench. I could see myself sitting alone on the park bench on the other side of the Event Horizon before events actually occurred and I could see those same events from where I was also now sitting after those same events occurred thus giving me the ability to see events coming before they happened and the results of those same events after they happened. As I sat there looking at myself from both locations I heard the music from the song 'Hands across the water' and the words, "HANDS ACROSS THE WATERS, HANDS ACROSS THE SEA"

When I returned to the original park bench no one was there so I went to where the Oracle lived over four thousand years in the past inside his cave. No one was there. I was alone and I was the Oracle. Then I went to where e-land was far in the future. What I thought was a control tower at an airport was in fact the command center of a giant space ship. The slanted glass windows were not windows at all but giant displays with picture perfect views of what lay outside. I was in a space ship and we were traveling through space. My name was Captain England and I was in command of a magnificent space ship.

Party bus

When I got back home it was almost 2:00 o'clock in the morning. I ran outside and saw the old school bus parked in front of my house with its doors swung open wide waiting for me. As I jumped onto the bus I asked Brad, the bus driver, where he was headed tonight. He said to the party. I wanted to know what party. Brad said this is the party bus and this is your party. The old bus was all decorated inside for a festive occasion and was full of all of my past and future lives. Everyone was cavorting and carrying on as the bus rolled along. I turned and looked ahead as the bus entered a shimmering transparent waterfall of some kind and everything dissolved as it entered.

On the other side I was left standing alone in the 'Place of Emptiness'. There was nothing anywhere. I was not in the 'Void' but I was in the 'Place of Infinite Possibilities'. I knew then that I was no longer a wizardling. I had just become a Wizard.

The next night I waited for the Night Bus to come at 2:00 o'clock in the morning. It never arrived. Then I waited for the gondola to come by at 3:00 a.m. It never showed up either. I guess a wizard doesn't need those things to travel on. After all, a wizard can go anywhere in the twinkle of an eye, any time he so chooses.

Blue Moon Two

A Blue Moon is the second full moon that occurs in a single month. This happens occasionally. It is unusual when there is more than one Blue Moon in a specific year. In the year 2018 there was a Blue moon in January and another one again in March. The last time there were two Blue Moons in a single year was

1999 and the next time that happens will be in the year 2037. The second full moon this year in March is supposed to come at 7:09 p.m. this evening on the 31st of March.

Last night when I went to 'The Place' to recharge my energy supply at 1:15 in the morning, the Source wanted me to go to where the Magic Crows were gathering for their monthly Full Moon meeting. I told the Source that I didn't know where the meeting was going to be held and besides that, the full moon wasn't supposed to be until this evening.

The Source said that he would take me there to where the Magic Crows were gathering in the Urals where it was already the full moon. He also told me that I would have to go as pure awareness so that I would be difficult for the Magic Crows to detect.

When I arrived I located the Spanish Crow. She is the only crow that still communicates with me. I whispered in her ear, "I am here, I am here, can you hear me?"

She said, "Where are you?"

I answered, "I am near. I am pure awareness. Where are we? Are we in the Ural Mountains in Russia? What year is it anyway?"

She said, "Quiet the other crows are looking at me. It is in the year 1917."

I watched quietly from atop the Spanish Crow's head as the monthly full moon gathering proceeded. I recognized the old crow wearing his pince-nez spectacles that brought their meeting to order. He said that for the first time their International 'Order of Magical Crows' had experienced a decline in their membership. No wonder, for sorcerers are a dying breed and sorcery is a dying art.

When I returned to 'The Place' to recharge once again, the Source told me that I needed to go see the 'Buddha on the Mountain'. So, I went there. When I entered the cave the Buddha asked me to come on his side of the fire-pit. Usually I sit on the opposite side of the pit facing the Buddha with the fire in between us. So I went to his side of the fire-pit and started to sit down facing the fire, which I always do. The Buddha asked me to sit facing him instead of the fire, so I did. I sat down with my legs crossed as though I were preparing to meditate. As I sat there facing the Buddha, I began to slowly rise up off of the ground until I was suspended in mid-air at the same level the Buddha was sitting in his chiseled out alcove. Then I began to move forward towards him until we merged into one being and I was looking out of the alcove at the fire-pit through his eyes.

A young boy about six years old entered the cave and approached me. He had dark hair and dark eyes. He was neither of light complexion nor dark complexion. He hugged me around the neck and said, "Thank you for releasing me so that I can begin my next life."

When I returned home I asked the Source what that experience was all about. He told me that I had been the 'Buddha on the Mountain' in another lifetime and that the boy was key to understanding this puzzle. I responded, "That must be why I am so weird." The Source said, "No, that is why you are capable of doing all the many things that others can never do."

Roberto Islas

The Source had said that the boy was key to my understanding the situation, so I went looking for him wherever that might end up being. Eventually I found him. He appeared to be a little bit older now, perhaps seven years of age. When I located him he was out in the countryside away from any roads or houses or other people. I asked him what his name was and he said Robert. I asked where he was born. He said Uruguay. I asked if he spoke Spanish. He said yes but we were communicating in English. Robert told me that he spoke both Spanish and English and when asked he told me that his last name was Islas and that he answered to both Robert or to Roberto.

I asked him when he was born. He said on the seventh day of the seventh month of the seventh year. That would make it on July seventh but the specific year was still in question. Robert told me he was born during the seventh year of his parent's marriage.

Joseph Silverstein

The Source told me more than one time that I need-ed to round up all of the characters from my alternate life experiences and to make a personal connection with each of them before I would be able to move on. Joseph Silverstein was one of the very last ones. When I found him he was very old. I explained to him what the situation was and he agreed to go with me through the "Door of No Return". We entered together but only I exited on the other side. I reached into my pocket and there were the two gold coins Joseph Silverstein had given me years ago. As I walked down the cobblestone road towards town I came upon several beggar chil-dren. I gave them the two gold coins for I knew that I would have had no use for them where I was going.

As I continued down the road I grew younger and younger. My clothing slowly changed. I ended up dressed as Tom Sawyer with a fishing pole over my shoulder and a can of worms in my hand. I had no shoes or shirt on, just a ratty old straw hat and old overalls that were two sizes too small. As I approached the river a large number of young women gathered around me. They were all of the many females that had accompanied me during my past lives. They all cried out for me to join them in the river.

As they entered the river they all were transformed into beautiful gold fish. Instead of walking into the river as they did, I walked above the surface of the water and when I reached the other side the landscape was totally barren. Nothing existed on the other side. I turned and looked back over the river and it had turned to sand. There was nothing but sand, the 'sands of time' as far as the eye could see.

When I stepped onto the land on the other side of the river it was transformed into the beautiful country-side where I met Robert Islas before. He was standing there alone. He asked, "Who are you, mister?" I said, "I don't know."

Robert said to me, "You see too much and know too little. I on the other hand know too much and see too little. Together we can see enough and know enough to get the job done."

Robert Islas said, "Together you can know more and I can see more." We held hands and he took me to where there was what looked like a bird's bath and he said for me to drink from it. I did so and a pathway appeared behind him. He said for us to go down the path together because it was a path that he could not see. We walked down the path holding hands and facing each other. He walked backwards and I walked forwards until we came to a fork in the road. He turned around and said that he could now see the path that diverged to the left but not the path that continued to the right.

Robert turned around and walked away down the pathway to the left and I turned and walked down the pathway to the right. It continued until it opened up into a clearing. The Source was waiting for me there. He said, "I see you finally made it." He asked me to walk with him. As we walked he said, "This is the 'Place of Knowing'. Here is where you come whenever you need to know something."

Dust of Time

After going to 'The Place' and recharging as I do daily, the Source asked me to walk with him. His arms were crossed behind his back and his hands were clasped together. As we walked slowly along the hard surface his feet kicked up dust. He said to me, "See this dust, it is the dust of time. It is not only the dust of time but time its self. Time is actually a thing. It actually has physicality. You can actually hold it in your hand. You can store it in a sack. It actually is sand-like. You can walk on it. You can form it into bricks, strange but true. Time does not exist as a solid in your reality or in your world but in other dimensions it does. As a seer, as a wizard, as a time traveler you are ready to make the leap into multiple dimensional realities and multidimensional worlds. That is the challenge that I give you." The Source vanished and I was alone in the vast emptiness.

One Octave, more or less

Last night when I was talking with the Source, I

told him that I had no idea how to gain access to other dimensions and realities. He suggested that the easiest point from which to gain access to other dimensional realities and worlds was from the 'Dream Scape'. He further advised me that since I am adept with manipulating time, I should keep time stationary and first modify the frequency at which I begin the process. He suggested that I first try a frequency one octave higher or one octave lower than the frequency of our own world and our own reality.

From my understanding, the term octave relates to sound and an octave is composed of eight notes with the difference between the frequency of the upper note and the lower note in the octave being either twice or half depending on whether you are going up the scale or down the scale in the octave. I think what the source was alluding to was not necessarily relative to sound but to the frequency or rate of oscillation of our world or our reality. That would require me to first determine precisely what that frequency is for our reality then doubling it or cutting it in half. At least that is a starting point for me to try to gain access to another world or another reality, which in fact might turn out to be superimposed upon our own reality.

Ebony & Ivory

Last night when I woke up I noticed an odd looking face in the corner of my field of vision on the right side. It looked like a combination of a normal face combined with a face built up out of Legos. The shape of the head was rectangular with a flat square lower jaw and a flat top of its head. The eyes were just round black balls. The eyebrows over the eyes were straight and black horizontal ribbons that were separated by a rectangular nose.

Instead of attempting to access another dimension or an alternate reality by going through the 'Dream Scape', I chose to go to the 'Place of Emptiness' and then to begin looking for the owner of the face from that starting point.

When I found that face, it belonged to a blonde male character that appeared to be almost human. When I asked him what his name was he told me that I could not even spell it let alone pronounce it so, I should just call him Ebony. He told me that he was indeed from another dimension, the frequency of which was one octave higher than our own dimension and that it occupied the same space as our dimension but on the opposite side of the waveform. He also informed me that the waveform that created his dimension as well as our own dimension was not sinusoidal but a square waveform like some inverters use. We exist on one side of the square waveform and they exist on the other side of that same square waveform but their dimension oscillates at twice the frequency as our dimension.

Our two dimensions are like the black and white keys being played next to each other on a piano and our two different dimensions are like two frequencies of two separate realities emitted from that same piano. The only way for me to accomplish this task was for me to become pure, disembodied awareness.

Sumuges

I checked in with the Source and asked what was next on his agenda for me. He told me to go down one octave to see what I could discover. Since I had no short cut like I did before with the face to use as an address in time and place I took the advice that the Source had given me about leaving from the 'Dream Scape'. When I found myself in the 'Dream Scape' last night I started looking for a way to engage the 'octave'.

I never hear anything per say while in the 'Dream Scape' but last night I distinctly heard a very low frequency sound. It was certainly loud enough that I was able to easily track the source of the sound to its point of origin.

The sound was definitely coming out of an arched doorway. More correctly it was an arched entrance way because it had no door and there was a continuation of a hall or perhaps better described, an arched tunnel that continued on the other side. The tunnel was the same size and the same shape as the entranceway. They were both constructed from large cut stones that looked like limestone or unpolished marble of off-white color. The tunnel sloped down at an angle. The floor consisted of eight steps that were about three inches in height and twenty to twenty-two inches wide. I walked down the steps. With each step the sound was lower and lower until when I reached the bottom of the tunnel there was no sound at all.

On the other side there were these little characters wandering around in pairs. They were like very small bipeds but definitely not humans. They had two legs and two arms. Their faces were concave and their two eyes were large and flat like discs. They had no hair. Each pair consisted of one member that was about twenty-two inches tall and the other about twenty inches tall. They were all dressed the same in medium gray tights with matching long sleeve shirts. The landscape was devoid of any trees or bushes but there was what we would probably call ground cover that was silver-gray like sagebrush. There were these strange looking objects all over the place. They looked like upside down acorns. The cap of the acorn-shaped objects were on the ground and the nut part of the acorn pointed straight up and looked like a giant egg. The color was white and the surface looked and felt like the surface of an egg. These things were as tall as the creatures walking around.

I assume that one of each pair could be what we think of as a male and the other could be what we consider a female but I don't know if that is actually the case. Likewise I assume that these egg-like acorns may in fact be a part of their reproductive cycle. This is all conjecture of course. I did manage to establish communications with one of these creatures. It told me that they were known as Sumuges. Well, so much for going down one octave.

Objectify

I was walking with the Source last night along a riverbank. He asked me to tell him what I saw. I have been to this same river many times in the past. This river is slow moving and straight. It is approximately seventy-five to one hundred feet wide. There is a nicely kept dirt pathway that runs along both sides of the river. Each time I have been here the river seemed to be the same. Only my experiences at the river have been different.

One time I was walking on both sides of the river at the same time. Another time I was walking on the near side of the river and swimming in the river at the same time. Another time I was walking on both sides of the river and swimming down stream at the same time. And yet again, another time I was observing myself swimming upstream while at the same time I was standing on the near side of the river noting that even though I was swimming continuously upstream, I was making no headway. I was merely staying stationary.

I shared those experiences with the Source. He said to me that the next time, I needed to be walking on both sides of the river at the same time and also swimming in both directions at the same time. No sooner had he mentioned that scenario, than I indeed found myself in the middle of the river swimming in both directions at the same time and also walking on both sides of the river in both directions at the same time without seeming to be making any headway at all.

The Source interrupted this experience and turned to me and said, "The River is actually time itself. Each of the different locations and directions of travel are different points of view. A point of view is the place from which you observe an event. A point of view has nothing to do with your opinion or personal beliefs.

If for example you broke your leg you would tend to think of that from a personal point of view. The goal is for you to not take whatever you encounter in life personally. You need to be able to relate to it as a broken leg and not as your broken leg. You need to experience the pain associated with the broken leg not as your pain but as pain that accompanies broken legs, just as you need to relate to the healing process not as your own personal healing but as the healing process associated with a broken leg. The only way you can 'not' take events and experiences you encounter on the journey of life personally is to objectify all of those experiences. Life is a temporary event. Life is a transitory event. Life is a transition not a permanent state. You must learn to objectify everything so you cannot take them personally."

River of Fire

11:39 p.m. I asked the Source, "What is it that you wish for me to do?"

Answer: "Come with me to the river."

Question: "What River is this?"

Answer: "The River of Fire. This is not a river of lava. No, this is the River of Fire, which separates Hades from Hell. You have been here before. Notice that the flames do nothing to you. That is because you are walking with me. These flames signify the limits of Hades and the limits of Hell. This River of Fire separates these two realities. Devils may not cross. Demons may not cross. You are mere awareness and as such are free to observe. Pass, as such you are free to travel safely with this River of Fire, safe from devils on your left, safe from demons on your right.

From this vantage point you can peer into the souls of evildoers and separate the devils from the demons. The demons can be reasoned with, the devils never. Look into their souls through this window. Devils will look back at you. Demons will welcome you into their beings. This window is the portal to the soul and can be seen and observed only from the River of fire". 12:02 a.m.

Isabella

On June 23rd, 2018 a little before 10:00 o'clock in the evening, we were in bed with the lights turned off for the night. My wife asked me if there was something in our bedroom. I told her I didn't know but I would check and see if I could find anything. Standing next to the bed, on her side, was what appeared to be a small girl less than three feet tall. I asked the small girl to come over to my side of the bed.

It is always challenging for me to determine what anything actually is in these situations. Eventually I ascertained that she was in fact a Fairy and she came bearing a gift for me. I accepted her gift graciously and asked if it were for Father's Day. Isabella was the name she gave me. The gift, she said, was not for Father's Day but for becoming the 'Wizard'. The gift she brought was the key to gain entrance to the world of Fairies. Isabella told me that the Fairies had no wizard and were in need of one. I asked her whom I should ask for when I go to the world of the Fairies. She said, "Isabella." After she delivered the key and her important message, she vanished in a shower of fairy dust. I told my wife to be sure and not vacuum the floor next to our bed because I wanted to get some Fairy dust if I could find any. Later that evening I followed Isabella's trail and gained entrance into Fairy Land using the key she gave me.

Isabella was there to greet me. She showed me this giant hole in the ground. It was easily twenty feet in diameter and was a perfectly round hole. Not an ordinary hole but a hole with no sides or bottom. It was a large hole filled with nothingness. Anything that fell into the hole simply disappeared. It wasn't even dark. It was like looking up at the sky when you peered into the hole. I have never seen anything like it before. Apparently it was my task as the newly installed wizard to somehow get rid of this strange thing.

The solution I came up with was to string a series of overlapping pieces of metal tubes open on one side forming a U in cross section completely around the perimeter of the hole. As I slowly pulled on the rope the tubes slid together further and further and the hole grew smaller and smaller until it finally disappeared and was completely gone as though I had sutured the earth back together with a giant draw-string. I was actually rather proud of my accomplishment. However: Isabella was quite upset at my apparent success. She told me that her best friend Mica had fallen into the hole and now there would be no way for him to get out... Another conundrum.

I retrieved a small stick from my satchel. It was from a branch of a cherry tree. I proceeded to pound it into the ground in the exact center of where the hole had been until the stick was completely buried in the ground. I stood back and the stick sprouted and began to grow into a gigantic cherry tree. I asked Isabella to carve Mica's name into the trunk of the tree. Then I scribed the outline of a door around his name and then embedded a brass handle into it where a doorknob should be. I asked Isabella to turn the handle and open the door. When she did so, Mica walked through the doorway and back into the land of the Fairies. Without so much as a thank you they ran off together in jubilation. I returned to my home and to my bed.

Out of nowhere a short, squat elf appeared at my bedside. He said that his name was Elmer. He presented me with a single red rose sent from Isabella in appreciation for rescuing her dearest friend Mica. As I accepted the single rose it transformed into a bouquet of red roses, obviously magical red roses from a beautiful fairy named Isabella.

Flanders Fields

I was walking with the Source last night. He asked me if I knew where we were. I told him that I had no idea where we were. He said, "In Flanders Fields". As we walked along wisps of smoke puffed out of the ground and shot up into the night sky. He asked if I knew what all those wisps of smoke were. Again I told him that I had no idea. The Source said they were the spirits of soldiers who died in World War I. He said that he had been here many times encouraging these many departed young soldiers to come out from hiding in their respective shallow graves but none would ever do so because they felt guilty and were too afraid of what the Source might do to them, to leave the safety of their respective graves but when I accompanied the Source, they quickly came forth and departed for their unknown futures because they felt safe in my presence. I have no idea why that would be the case.

After the Source departed, leaving me alone in Flanders Fields, I continued to walk the entire area where all of these spirits have remained for the past hundred years. With my passing they continued to pour forth from beneath the green grasses, where poppies once grew, in Flanders Fields.

I chanced upon the grave of one, Tyler Moore, dead by age seventeen. That seemed very young to me to come to the end of one's life so violently and so young. I was drawn to this particular grave by a sense of great sadness and futility. As I contemplated Tyler's passing at such a young age I sensed movement out of the corner of one eye. I asked perchance could that be the ghost of Tyler Moore. The answer came back as a yes. He lied to get into the army and died not as the hero he envisioned but as a gut-shot kid sorrowful and fearful of death's coming. He never forgave himself for the untold sadness his pointless demise inflicted upon his mother and his friends. I assured him that they were all now, long since dead and buried and surely awaiting his arrival where they would rejoice at his homecoming. Excited he departed, last of all in leaving Flanders Fields, where poppies once grew.

Coyote's Howl

It was September 24th, the night of the Harvest Moon. It was after midnight. I was talking with the Source. As we walked along in the light from the full moon he said to me that he was giving me the 'Gift of Life'. I heard a coyote's mournful howl in the distance. I was very excited to receive the 'Gift of Life'. What a magnificent gift to share with others. He then told me that with the 'Gift of Life' came the 'Curse of Death'. I was very distraught because that was the last thing I wanted to have. I told the Source that I could never be trusted with the 'Curse of Death', for surely I would begin killing all of those I felt were justly deserving of such a fate. The Source elaborated, "There is no good without evil. There is no Yin without Yang." He said that I must decide for he would not again offer to bestow this 'Gift of Life' upon me. I didn't know what to do. What a magnificent gift... What a horrible curse.

The coyote howled three times. It was closer now. I went to visit the coyote and shape-shifted myself into a coyote and sat down in front of it in the moonlight. I shared my dilemma with the Wise and Wiley coyote. He said that I must accept the gift that was offered to me. When I complained about the curse that accompanied this gift. He said, "A dog without a bite is all bark, and not a real dog at all." I returned and informed the Source that I would accept the "Gift of Life" The coyote howled three times. The Source then gave me the 'Curse of Death." The coyote howled six times and my Fate was sealed. I asked the Source if the gift of life could be bestowed upon another person from a distance. He said that the 'Gift of Life' could only be transferred by touch because life is a physical state but the 'Curse of Death' could be delivered by coming out from within the dreamscape like Freddy Kruger, for death is a non-physical state.

A couple of hours later, I heard the coyote howl mournfully in the distance. My wife began to shake and gasp for breath in her sleep. I was afraid she might be dying. I touched her. I shared the 'Gift of Life' with her and she returned to a peaceful state of sleep. In the distance, the coyote howled twice with seeming satisfaction.

In the morning, my wife shared a strange dream she had during the night. She said that she was at a gathering where two of her great uncles greeted her happily with hugs and adulation. She asked them if they knew who she was, for she had not seen them since she was a young girl. They said of course they knew who she was. There were several other people gathered there as well. All of them now long since dead and buried.

The Pasture

Last night the Source took me to a place he called the "Pasture". He asked me to tell him what I saw. I have never seen anything that was remotely similar to what I was observing. There was an expansive flat space where there were vertical striations emitting from the ground. They were narrow, all different in color, in pattern and in frequency of vibration. The colors were not brilliant but subdued. I had no idea what these things were. I knew the Source was pushing me to go beyond any self-imposed limitations. I summoned the wizard's powers of observation and this is what I saw:

The striations disappeared and out of the dusky background emerged an Indian, bare-chested in long leather jerkins and simple moccasins. His hair was long, dark and braided and there was one feather canted off to one side. I recognized him at first sight as the spirit shape-shifting coyote. He stopped and stood all the way to the left side and became the coyote. Next came the spirit deer, then the bear, the wolf, the hawk, the eagle, the elk, the skunk, the raccoon, one by one until all the spirit animals of Indian myth and religion had emerged and shape shifted into their spirit animal form. I went out to meet them.

One by one I shape shifted into each of the different animals and greeted them as brothers. When that process was completed they all vanished and the "Pasture" became an inland expanse of water. One by one it populated with all of the spirit creatures of the lakes and rivers and sea. When all of the water spirits were assembled I greeted them individually and shape shifted into their animal forms. After I greeted each and all, everything disappeared and I was standing alone next to the Source in an expansive verdant alpine meadow ringed with pine and fir and white aspen. The Source asked me if I understood what I had just experienced. My answer:

"How do I get people to understand?"

Stone Dragon & Fetch

I was in the 'dream scape' last night walking in a desert arroyo when I passed a sentry-dog on the other side of a metal gate. The gate was not connected to a fence, just a driveway size Cyclone gate with no fence on either side. The dog was a large German shepherd police dog. It was running back and forth on the other side of the gate, barking like crazy. I was sure it was going to attack me. I wrapped my handkerchief around the knuckles on my right hand in preparation for a fight that I knew was imminent. The dog ran around the right end of the gate and came at me full speed.

As I crouched and turned to face him, he sailed right past me and ran straight to a large boulder about twenty feet away in the middle of the arroyo. He jumped against the boulder with his front paws and the rock was transformed into a 'Stone Dragon', not a fire-breathing dragon with wings but it was more like a very large, fat alligator with long legs. The dog sat down next to the stone dragon, stared at me, panting with his tongue lolling out from all his exertion. I had no idea what was going on. So I decided that I needed to ask the dragon.

I sat down directly in front of the stone dragon that was now moving his head all about. When I asked who he was and who the dog was and what the point was of this whole experience, the dragon told me that he was the 'Stone Dragon' and the German shepherd was named 'Fetch'. He said that whenever I was at a loss for a word to describe something exactly the way it should be described I should ask Fetch and he would come to the stone in the arroyo and jump up on it and the 'Stone Dragon' would emerge from the rock and give Fetch that perfect word I was looking for and Fetch would bring the perfect word back to me so that I could describe it perfectly. The police dog fetches whatever word I need from the Stone Dragon. That is why he is called 'Fetch'.

Little Bear

Yesterday morning I took the trash from the kitchen out to the alley behind our house and tossed it into the large, green, communal trash container. On my way back I noticed that someone had trimmed the grass around our water-meter box and raked the cuttings into a circle about three-feet in diameter around the meter-cover. I have never seen that done before and we have lived in this house forty-five years. About two feet away from the water-meter is a large pine-tree with a trunk about eighteen inches in diameter.

Last night while I was talking with the Source, my visual field was suddenly filled with the water-meter scene and the large pine-tree trunk. Just behind the meter-cover and next to the pine-tree I saw the snout of a small brown bear. I got down on my hands and knees and crawled over to where the small bear was hiding. It turned and moved back into the shadows. I scurried after it and found myself in the middle of the prairie in thick buffalo grass. There standing in front of me was a young Indian boy about ten years of age. I recognized him as the boy that I have had other adventures with in the past. He was wearing deerskin jerkins and moccasins. He had long, dark, hair tied neatly back in a ponytail and he was shirtless. I assumed that I was also a young boy like I had been in other adventures with him. On one previous occasion I had been an Indian boy and on another occasion I had been an Anglo. I looked at my hands. They were bear-paws, covered in thick, brown fur.

As we stood there in the tall prairie grass, the boy grew older and became a young man then an older man and finally he became a chief wearing a full, feathered headdress. At that point he sat down in a small circular clearing in front of a fire-pit with rocks around it. He lit a fire then put dry grass into the fire until smoke began billowing up into the sky. I climbed into the smoke as it rose slowly upwards and I became a man once again. The Indian Chief climbed up into the smoke after me. As he climbed inside the smoke he was transformed into a bear. I asked him what his name was and he said, "Little Bear." I asked the bear what my name was and he said, "Traveler...You are the traveler."

We talked briefly about the nature and purpose of the smoke. He told me that to an Indian, smoke reveals the true nature and form of everything. Then, I asked him who he actually was. He said that he was "Little Bear" and that this was his true form. He was a bear. Then I asked him who I was and he said, "You are 'Druid', I am 'Little Bear'".

Big Boy, Weasel & Pudd

Yesterday my son who lives in California called with a problem he wanted me to take care of. His black cat, Indy, has been urinating on the carpet in the hall instead of using one of the three litter boxes or just going outside. I told him that I would see what I could do but I have never dealt with a problem like that before so I would probably need to get help from someone to resolve this problem.

While I was working on a project with the Source I asked if he knew of anyone who might help out with my son's cat problem. The Source never answered my question.

Late in the morning around 3:30 a.m., I was in the dream state with my wife. We were at a movie theater waiting for the film to begin. I was sitting in an aisle seat. She was sitting next to me. The seat next to her was unoccupied. My wife left to get some popcorn at the snack bar. I was supposed to save her seat. A young woman and her boyfriend pushed their way into the seats and sat down. I told the young woman that I was saving that seat for my wife who had gone to the concession stand for some refreshments. She said that

258

she didn't care. She didn't buy into that 'seat saving routine' and she wasn't going to leave.

Her boy friend was big and so was she. I didn't know what to do because my wife would soon return and I would be in big trouble. At that moment three dogs descended from nowhere and started jumping all over the woman next to me. One was a black and brown wiener-dog, one was a black mutt and the third was a giant police dog. He had to weigh at least two hundred pounds. He stuck his butt right in her face and raised his tail. The other two dogs were jumping all over her boyfriend licking and scratching him. The guy and his girl friend both got up and left before my wife returned.

I asked the big dog what his name was. He said, "Big Boy." The mutt's name was Weasel and the dachshund was called Pudd. I got the idea that they might be the answer to the cat's peeing problem. They agreed to go to my son's house and keep the black cat Indy out of the hallway and stop him from peeing anywhere but in the litter boxes.

I opened a portal to my son's house and we all arrived safely together. They eagerly took up their sentry duty keeping Indy in line.

Sugar-Plums

For the past couple of weeks the Source has been ushering me through a project that is challenging for me. Not that all of his requests aren't difficult for me to work through but this one has been especially hard for me to grasp. For the first step in this process the Source took me to a place where there was essentially nothing. He raised his right arm and in a sweeping motion from due east to southwest he said, "This is your realm. This is your domain." I didn't see anything.

I asked what he was referring to. He said that it had nothing to do with cardinal direction as in east or west or up or down or space or property but purely with reality. He left me standing there confused.

A week later he repeated the process extending the range from 120 degrees to 220 degrees, from east to northwest. Again he left me standing there alone and confused. Last night the Source swept his arm in a complete circle and said that all of it was now my realm. All of it was now my domain. Here I was capable of understanding all realities. I found that hard to believe.

Where moments before there was nothing now was filled with sugarplums dangling down on threads. He never told me anything about the sugarplums. They were very large and delicious looking. I reached out and grasped the one closest to me. The other sugarplums vanished. A long column of pictures appeared lined up in domino fashion. They snaked their way towards me from my left side then wrapped around me and continued off to the right where they abruptly ended.

Inside each frame was a picture of me. The first one

was of a newborn baby the last one was of a very old man. There must have been a hundred of them. The one closest to me reflected me at my present age. I picked up the first picture and all of the other pictures vanished except the second photograph. In between the two, which were apparently one year apart, eleven more pictures appeared, one for each month of that first year.

I picked up the first and second photos that were taken one month apart and photos appeared for each week of my life. I picked up the first two photos and pictures of each day of that first week appeared. Then, I picked up the two photos of my first day of life and photos for each hour of that day appeared, then for each minute of that first hour. I finally understood what sugarplums really are.

They contain all of the memories of a person's life.

The River

The other night I was conversing with the Source as we were walking along together, when he stopped, looked straight at me and said, "It's time." We proceeded for a ways further until we came to the edge of a river. There wasn't a riverbank and there was no vegetation anywhere. There was just plain brown dirt and plain brown water separated by a knife-edge juncture between the water and the dirt.

He said to me, "This is the river." I could barely

detect a very slow movement of the water in the river, but just barely. The surface was flat and smooth and the river was very wide. I couldn't make out the other side clearly. It was too far away.

The Source said, "This is the river of time. To the left is the future. To the right is the past. Right in front of us is the present. If you walk on the ground on the edge of the river in either direction, when you turn to face the river it will always be the present. If you walk on the surface of the river itself to your right you will move into the past. If you walk to your left on the surface of the river it will always be the present because no mater at what pace you proceed up river, the flow of the river will always match the speed at which you walk up stream keeping you always in the present moment.

If you go over to the other side of the river, facing us, you can walk into the future or into the past by walking on the ground next to the river. If you walk to your left you will move into the future and if walk to your right you will walk into the past. The further you walk on the edge of the river, the further you move forward or backwards in time, when you turn and face the river.

The challenge is in getting over to the other side of the river of time. You cannot walk across on the surface of the river and you cannot go by portal because on this side of the river time moves in one direction and on the other side of the river times moves in the opposite direction. The only way for you to get to the other side is to use the 'Black Door to Anywhere'". He vanished leaving me standing at the edge of the 'River of Time'

Spectrum

One night in the past, when I checked in with the Source, he began walking and wanted to re-visit the topic of fog and smoke. He reminded me that fog and smoke were created by un-certainty. He then pointed out the absence of fog and smoke as we walked towards the abyss. "You have obviously devised a way to manage uncertainty effectively", he said. "You are ready now to see the Spectrum. In front of you is the abyss. You can see the edge where what we are walking on meets the abyss. To the right is the Place of Emptiness. To the left is the Void. If you put your hand into the Place of Emptiness it will disappear, for there is nothing physical in the Place of Emptiness. If you put your hand into the Void, your hand will still exist and your spectrum will also exist, there in that 'Void'.

A spectrum appeared like a giant rainbow in the void. The Source said, "The spectrum is a reflection of indifference, your indifference. It appears as your spectrum in the Void." The spectrum that appeared in front of me from within the abyss was absent many of its bars of color. It was incomplete.

"Your task is to complete the spectrum and fill the

blank spaces with their missing colors. Then you will no longer bear the burden of indifference." The Source disappeared leaving me alone to contemplate on how to abandon my personal indifferences and to thereby restore my spectrum in its entirety.

That encounter happened quite some time ago. Last night I returned to the 'Wizards Bridge'. I crossed over the bridge and on the other side I met up with many of my past lives. We formed a circle and merged into a singularity. My spectrum re-appeared. It was now almost complete. Apparently this technique is effective in compensating for my own personal indifferences.

Black Door

Last night I was talking with the Source in 'The Place'. He asked me to recharge there with the maximum amount of energy that I could because he wanted to show me something afterwards. When I finished recharging he wanted me to completely clear my mind of any thoughts and then to stop my internal dialog. At that point he outlined a black door with wide, bold, lines. He asked me what I thought it was. I told him that I didn't know. He proceeded to fill the outline in completely. It looked like a large upright rectangle to me. He said, "This is a door."

It had no hinges and no knob or handle. He re-iterated, "This is a door. This is your door. Only you can open this door. Only you can use this door. It will take you anywhere, to any place, to any time, to any reality, to any universe."

Then he presented me a key on a gold chain and placed it around my neck. Being the skeptic that I am I asked where I should put the key since the door had no lock and no Knob, no hinges and no handle. And then I asked what if someone took the key away from me. At that instant the gold chain and the key itself sank deep into my chest and neck and the Source said, "You are the key. You and only you can open this door to anywhere." I was left standing alone in front of a large black door with no visible hinges, no handles and no locks.

Barrier of Disbelief

Last night at midnight, after I recharged myself at "The Place", the Source asked me to walk with him. He asked me to tell him what I saw. We were walking on a solid flat surface that had a narrow stream of what resembled water. It was flowing in the same direction as we were walking. It was only about six or seven inches wide and was clear without a lot of turbulence as though the surface we were walking on had a groove in it and was sloped slightly downhill. The stream was moving at about the same rate as we were walking. Outside of that stream I wasn't aware of anything.

I obviously fell off the wagon, as one might say and went to sleep. When I awoke it was three o'clock in the morning. I was still walking along that same stream with the Source. Before long another similar stream appeared ahead of us on the left, which was flowing perpendicular to the stream we were following. We stopped where the two streams intersected. The two streams did not seem to mix as they crossed. The new stream, which was approximately the same size as the first stream, crossed over the other stream and under it.

The Source told me that the first stream was the 'stream of consciousness'. The second stream was the 'stream of awareness' and where the two streams crossed was the 'barrier of disbelief.' On the other side lies the 'manifestation of reality.' He told me that I must move beyond the 'barrier of disbelief', which was blocking my progress.

I asked the Source if I were ever going to become a great seer and a great healer. He said that I have always been a seer and I have always been a healer. The only thing that stood in my way was the 'barrier of disbelief', which I must now overcome.

Reality

Last night the Source took me to a place where there wasn't anything that I could see. He stretched out his arm like Elasta-girl and asked me to tell him what he was pointing at. His arm zoomed off into the distance far over the horizon. My eyes followed his hand closely. It stopped at a place where there was a circular spot on the floor that was illuminated. Sitting in the middle of the circle of light was an infant wearing only a diaper. He appeared normal in every way except for his head, which was large and round with only one hair on its otherwise baldhead. The baby had one single tooth that was very large like a beaver. From there, the Source stretched his arm off in another direction. My vision followed closely until we stopped at a hole in the ground. The hole was no more than eight inches deep and eight inches in diameter. There was nothing in the hole and nothing around it either. The Source asked me to describe what I saw, so I did. Once again the Source stretched his arm far off in another direction. Again my vision followed along until we came to an abrupt stop. There was a very small zebra the size of a small goat. After I described what I saw to the Source, his arm zoomed off again in a different direction. His hand stopped at a very small round green bush with tiny round green leaves. The Source asked me to describe what I saw to him.

From there, we went back to where we had initially started. The Source then asked me to go through that same process on my own. The only address I had for each of the places we had visited was my memory of each separate place. I couldn't go by portal because I didn't have a compete address. After I went to each place in the exact order that we had just done, I revisited the infant and then took the little boy and left him with the small zebra before going back to where the Source was.

The Source told me that in the past everywhere I had traveled was located some where in time and space. But tonight I had traveled in reality, which was an entirely different aspect of address.

Confidence Window

A couple of nights ago the Source showed me a very large picture frame. It was four feet in height and seven feet in width. He referred to it as a window. He said that this window would allow an observer to view any event in the past, present or future with a degree of certainty. He left it at that for me to try and figure out how to use it. It was not a window as we might think of a window. It was a large frame for a picture suspended in mid-air with no picture and no glass in it. You could look right through it and see everything on the other side. I worked on this frame project for quite a while but it was obvious to me that I was getting nowhere.

Last night the Source took me back to where the window was located and explained to me how it worked. On the left side of the frame a little more than half way up from the bottom was a small invisible door that opened out and to the left. There was some buttons and a display behind this door. Here you were supposed to enter the degree of certainty in percentage points that you desired.

On the opposite side of the frame there was another secret door that opened to the right and exposed more buttons and another display. Here you were supposed to enter the date and time of the event that you wanted to observe.

On the top of the window frame in the center, there was a third secret door that opened upwards. Here you were supposed to enter the name of the person and the specific event in question.

The fourth secret door was located in the center of the bottom frame of the window. It opened downward and had only three options from which you could choose. The top choice was the reality of that person associated with that particular happening or event. The second choice was your own personal reality or point of view. The third choice was the actual reality of that event.

I tried it out a few times. It seemed to work fairly well but the higher the degree of certainty you requested, the more difficult the task is to complete.

Sense of Self

My son called yesterday in the evening and said that there was something in his house. He didn't know what it was or where I should look for it but something was making his daughter and his wife both act weird.

I asked him where they had gone during the day. He said they went to a museum that was being renovated so they were only able to go into the exhibit for trains. I told him that I would be over later.

I didn't know whether I should go it alone or organize an expeditionary group to deal with an unknown challenge. I asked the Source for his input. He suggested I go alone initially to get some idea what I would be dealing with. So, after midnight I ventured over to his house as pure awareness. I asked the tree spirit dogs that were on guard duty there at my son's house if there were anything anywhere in the house. They all said that there was nothing anywhere in the house.

If there was nothing in the house then the next place to look was the museum they visited during the day. Since the museum was being renovated there is no way for me to know what kind of disturbances the renovation process created. Once I was there it didn't take me long to find a part of my granddaughter huddled in a corner. I took her back to my son's house and put her in bed with the rest of her. Then, I went back to the museum looking for my son's wife. Sure enough I found her or some part of her in one of the rooms in an antique railway display. I repeated the process and took her back to her house and put her in bed with the rest of her. I assumed that they would reintegrate naturally without my intervention but that remains to be determined.

Apparently when my granddaughter and her mother

visited the museum, they had somehow lost part of themselves. They had lost the "Sense of Self". I had merely retrieved their missing parts and returned them to the rightful owners.

Gecko Tails

Last night when I woke up at 2:21 a.m., I saw an eye in the left side of my field of vision. It had a pupil with a vertical slit like a snake. There has always been some adventure waiting for me on the other side of every eye that I have encountered. All you have to do is catch the eye and enter into it through the pupil to discover what lies beyond.

When I passed through the pupil of the eye what I saw was a short fat worm that was dancing around like crazy. The next thing that appeared was a gecko. It was standing on its back legs right in front of me staring right at me. We were both about the same size. When I asked the gecko about the dancing worm, the one worm suddenly multiplied into a whole bunch of dancing worms framing the gecko like a picture. The gecko informed me that they were not dancing worms but fat dancing gecko tails.

I asked the gecko what the reason was for all the dancing gecko tails. The gecko told me that whenever a gecko is frightened it jettisons its tail, which then squirms all over the place, while the gecko makes its escape to safety. The gecko must obviously have thought that I was very dangerous so I shape shifted into a gecko myself. One by one the dancing gecko tails began to disappear. I informed the gecko that I was a shape shifter and posed no threat to it. The Gecko doubted my story. So, I told him that I was an exact duplicate of the gecko itself, not a mirror image but an exact duplicate. My right side was the same as its right side. The gecko then elaborated on its perspective of the world, which is very different from my own life's experiences as a top predator. The gecko is a formidable nighttime predator in its own world of insects and worms. I asked, in passing, about seeing the world through slit-like pupils like a devil has.

The gecko said that you could easily distinguish between a gecko and a devil's eye because when you look into the pupil of a devil you see tiny turbulent bubbles, fire and flames. When you look into the pupil of a gecko you see only dancing gecko tails.

Golden, Rod

Last night I saw an eye, a small eye, in the periphery of my visual field. Eyes are always portals to somewhere so I make a point of trying to catch hold of an eye and make entrance through it to see where it can take me. There was this shadowy outline of a tall thin man on the other side of the eye. When I passed through the eye into the inner workings beyond, there was a shimmering curtain-like membrane. On the other side of the curtain I could see the tall thin man that made the shadow.

He and his clothes were completely metallic gold in color. I caught his attention and asked what his name was. He told me that his name was Rod. I asked Rod where we were and what the shimmering membrane was for. He told me that I was in the realm of probability and the curtain was the shimmering curtain of certainty that separated the realm of probability from the place of infinite possibilities where he was located. The only thing I saw there in the place of infinite possibilities was a small wood desk made of oak. I asked Rod, the golden man, if I could come over to where he was in the place of infinite possibilities. He told me that I could come over but if I did so I would never be able to return to the realm of probability but would forever remain in the place of infinite possibilities. I didn't hesitate at all before I passed through the shimmering curtain of certainty. When I got to the other side I noticed that there was indeed nothing at all there in the place of infinite possibility. Rod, the golden man, told me that I had to create everything out of my own imaginings but there were absolutely no limitations on what I could be create or become if I chose to do so. I knew for certain then that this was my kind of place.

Follow Me

Last night when I talked with the Source he said, "Follow me." He has never asked me to follow him before. That was the first time, so I followed him. We seemed to be walking inside of a transparent tube. At first I thought that the tube sloped downward as we walked but in fact the tube was shrinking as we walked and as the tube shrank so did the Source and so did I. As we walked down the tube everything outside of the tube appeared to be getting bigger and bigger.

We were being miniaturized more and more as we continued down the tube. We passed through the molecular world, the sub-atomic world and the particle world until eventually the Source and I both no longer existed. He stopped and I stopped. We were both nothingness yet we continued to communicate clearly with each other even though neither of us existed from a physical perspective at all. "You have followed me here by faith. Faith is knowing. Faith is extrinsic in nature. Faith is immutable. Faith can move mountains.

Believing is intrinsic. Beliefs are changeable. Beliefs come from within.

Faith is unchangeable. It comes from God. You have followed me from the transient 'there' to the immutable here, to this, the place of nothingness, to this, the place of emptiness, to this the place of infinite possibilities."

The Precipice

3:14 a.m., June 7, 2018. The Source said, "Come with me. I want to take you to the Precipice. This is where your reality ends and other realities begin. This is where sorcery ends and wizardry begins.

The sorcerer is supposed to leap into the abyss and hopefully survive. The wizard is supposed to transcend or go over the abyss. The precipice is the end of the known and the beginning of the unknown. To the sorcerer this is the beginning of the unknowable, which in essence is the beginning of the unpredictable for the wizard. This is the end of sorcery and the beginning of the changeable.

Change begins on the underside of Wizard Island where the imaginings sprinkle down like floating dewdrops from the tree of existence. These imaginings are not your imaginings but the imaginings of creation. You can become a chooser and start these imaginings on their journey to becoming reality. These imaginings are free for the choosing by a wizard. Choose wisely and also un-choose wisely for your choices will become reality."

3:30 a.m.

Books published by Queens Army LLC

'Robin' Published April 2018
  ISBN # 978-1-940985-55-8
  Copyright 2018
  Library of Congress # 2018932795
  This is a book of Elizabethan poetry.
  By: Sonja Sjorgensen

'Oracle' Published December 2018
  ISBN # 978-1-940985-95-4
  Copyright 2018
  Library of Congress # 2018908403
  By: Dr. Michael T. Mayo

Other Books by Dr. Mayo

The trilogy of '**Coincidental Journey**', '**Untold Story**' & '**Wizardling**', pertain to lucid dreaming, dream walking, shape-shifting, magic, Sorcery, Wizardry, time-travel and the power of illusion. These three books are completed but a release date for this trilogy is pending translation into Spanish.

'**Coincidental Journey**'   Copyright 2015
    ISBN # 978-1-940985-16-9
'**Untold Story**'   Copyright 2016
    ISBN # 978-1-940985-42-8
'**Wizardling**'   Copyright 2017
    ISBN # 978-1-940985-73-2

'**Star Quest: Navigator**'
    ISBN # 978-1-940985-74-9
    This book is being finished. It evaluates several earth-like exo-planets located within habitable zones of their star systems for possible future human colonization.   Completion date is pending.

'**I, Druid**'   Completion date is pending.
"**1937**"   Completion date is pending.
'**Vision Quest**' Completed in 2018.   Awaiting publication and release.
'**The Art of Magic**' Completion date is pending.

About the Author

Dr. Mayo was born in Tucson, Arizona. He maintains a private dental practice located in the heart of Tucson which is limited to the treatment of children and special-needs patients.

CPSIA information can be obtained
at www.ICGtesting.com
Printed in the USA
FSHW020155090420
68980FS

9 781940 985732